Hamp & Mary Bibb

THE BEGINNING

James H. Ware Jr.

Order this book online at www.trafford.com
or email orders@trafford.com

Most Trafford titles are also available at major online book retailers.

Print information available on the last page.

ISBN: 978-1-4907-6024-7 (sc)
ISBN: 978-1-4907-6025-4 (e)

Library of Congress Control Number: 2015907668

Trafford rev. 05/12/2015

 www.trafford.com
North America & international
toll-free: 1 888 232 4444 (USA & Canada)
fax: 812 355 4082

Contents

PREFACE

Memories are not like historical records that progress along an uninterrupted time line. They are more like computer games and jigsaw puzzles, they do not continue in straight lines. They move by association; one memory triggers another and so on. In one sense what you will be reading is an autobiography (my story as I remember it), but it is more than that. It includes a sage of a family which reaches out six generations and encompasses a cluster of clans, cousins, and significant people who are inseparably intertwined in my recall. Like any work of memory it is full of biases. It is probably full of factual errors, although I have tried to confirm the accounts that I have narrated from old letters, family trees, stories told over the dinner table, and the memory of others who participated in the events. To say that it is a work of imagination would not be wrong, but it is an imagination which works though the mind's eye and records the images of memory and family lore.

This is the first of a number of volumes. It covers the years prior to Hamp and Mary Bibb going to China, their arrival in China and marriage, and the first few years of their missionary life in China. The entire series of Hamp

James H. Ware Jr.

and Mary Bibb biographies goes up to their departure to Hawaii in 1950.

The primary sources for the information about Hamp and Mary Bibb are the letters which Bibb wrote to her mother from the beginning of her life in China. Her mother saved many of these letters, and I found them in an old Chinese camphor chest in the old home place in Tupelo, Mississippi. Hamp and Bibb do not fit the stereotype of Southern Baptist. Bibb was far more conservative than Hamp, but neither of them were racist southerners. They were from elite professional families. Their parents were college graduates. Bibb's mother went to college at Mississippi State College for Women in the 1800s, Her father was a lawyer and District Judge in the First District Court in Mississippi. Hamp's father was a physician who had gone to medical school in Atlanta, Georgia. Shortly after the U. S. Civil War. Both had college undergraduate degrees and some graduate work including seminary for Hamp and Women's Missionary Union for Bibb.

Very little attention has been paid to the numerous young Americans who went to China just after World War I. They were exceptional people who were willing to go into an unknown land and live and work with the Chinese people who were undergoing the greatest changes of any modern people. I hope that the reader will not only find their lives informative, but also inspiring.

CHAPTER ONE

Hamp

A pink marble obelisk rises from the little hillock that dominates the cemetery in old Duluth, Georgia. It has been there for over a hundred years, a monument to love. A three-foot square polished block rises to about shoulder high from the wide chiseled marble base. Above the central block a round tapering column rises another ten feet and is topped off with an urn like cap that adds another two feet to the spire. Sometime in the past fifty years a walnut tree has grown up to half hide the top of the column and shade the pink stone. It's splintered and partly decayed trunk shows signs of numerous lightening strikes. The tree grew up through the gravel of the narrow cemetery road that borders one side of the family plot. Knobs have healed over here and there where it has been trimmed up to let hearses bring their burdens to other parts of the hillside. The white lap sided building that was once the Baptist church still stands on the north side of the cemetery. Looking in any other direction, there is not much left to see but derelict homes and rundown neighborhoods. But, to me, this is where it all begins, with the people who have been laid to rest within the granite borders of the family plot and the community of friends departed.

My grandfather, Elisha Green Ware, moved to Duluth from Walnut Grove, Georgia shortly after my father was born. Within a year, my Grandmother, Emily Robena Carter, died in childbirth and the pink marble obelisk was raised with it first roughly cut inscription:

Erected
In Memory of Precious
Emily Robena
Daughter of
James W.& Laura Carter
Wife of Dr. E.G. Ware
Born Dec. 4 1864
And fell asleep in Jesus
July 12, 1896
As a daughter, she was obedient and good.
As a wife, she was perfection.
As a mother, she was positive and firm,
patient, kind, gentle and loving.
As a Christian, she was earnest, devoted, faithful, and true.

I had seen the obelisk before; when my father and I stopped by to pay our respects at the family shrine. It stood out, caught your eye, in a field of stone bordered family lots and gray headstones. But it had been standing there for seventy five years before I read its message. Love was in my father's house. It sloshed between the members. It was sentimental, lavish, joyful, immediate, and lasting. It was responsible and loyal in life and in death. That was the way it was, and it was inconceivable in my father's family for it to be otherwise. There was nothing pretentious, arrogant, or ingenuous about it. It was like laughter that filled all the distances between them.

My father was two years old when my grandmother died leaving three young children. Viola was the oldest. Samuel David Hawthorn, who was two years older than my father, was next. My father, James Theodore Hamilton Carter, was the youngest. My grandfather had a penchant for giving his children family names even if it meant that they would each have four or five. Viola became more than a sister to the boys; she became the female head of the house. Probably the most influential woman in the children's lives was Aunt Charity, the cook that lived with the family until the household was broken up. She was really the children's surrogate mother. Until I recently learned about Aunt Charity's role, I never quit understood why my father gave our Chinese ahma (nurse maid) so much latitude in my upbringing. Both brothers became known by their third names, Hawthorn and Hamilton. Although Hamilton, or Hamp, as he was known most of his life, was the youngest of the three, he seems to have had a great deal of influence over his siblings. In later life they not only loved him, but idolized him.

As a child, I heard very little about my grandfather, accept that he was a physician, and nothing about my grandmother Ware. My first real knowledge of him came after my own mother's death when my father came to live with us in Staunton, Virginia for a short time. One week we drove down through the mountains of North Carolina into the foothills of North Georgia to visit Duluth. It was homecoming for my Dad, a time to pass on memories and

3

a legacy. We came into town down old highway U.S. 29, which was still two lanes, turned across the railroad tracks, moved down the rows of red brick storefronts that seemed to stand at parade rest as we passed by. Like so many old graying towns that straddled the railroad, the buildings reflected an era that was not only passed, but almost forgotten. A few buildings were still in use. Others were empty, boarded up, or in such bad repair that no one still cared for them. As my Dad reminisced aloud everything came alive as we drove down Main Street and then explored the roads west of town where the family farm had once been. He showed me a house that was a duplicate of the old home place, and we went back and forth passing the newer homes and the new stone Baptist church until finally we came back to town and the old cemetery.

According to the lore in Mathews County, Virginia, five Ware brothers arrived on the western bank of Chesapeake Bay sometime before the American Revolution. There are still places like Ware's Warf, Ware's Neck, and Ware's Church in the area. One of the Wares, Lt. Edward Ware, was born in Amherst County, Virginia in 1760. He married Sarah Thurmond. Edward and enlisted in the Revolutionary Army at the age of sixteen. His brother James also fought in the Revolutionary Army and was sighted for bravery in the field by General Washington after the battle of Yorktown. Edward Ware seems to have served as a Private, a Sergeant (sic), a Brevet, and a Second Lieutenant. He fought in battles at Guilford and York. After the Revolution he moved to Madison County, Georgia where he amasses a small fortune. In his Will he gave each of his eleven children a horse and a saddle, and, much to my chagrin, a slave. Three of the five brothers left

Virginia and ended up in what is now Georgia, Louisiana, and Texas. Of course, they were all Anglicans. Henry Ware, one of George's sons, was a strong Presbyterian and opposed immersion. His wife joined a Baptist Church; there were no Presbyterian Churches near her. Henry told her that he would shoot the preacher when he immersed her. However, after advising with his mother, his wife was baptized and Henry did not shoot the minister, but cried.

My great grand father Asa Jones Ware was born in 1813 and out lived three of his wives. He was first married to Francis Bird by whom he had two children and five grandchildren. Following her death Asa married Mary Ann Hood, my great grandmother, and had three children, the last of the three by her was my grandfather, Elisha Green Ware. William Ware, the second child of this marriage, and his wife, Cornelia McElhannan, had nine children and at least six grand children. This is not particularly unusual for the times, because there was a shortage of men after the Civil War; but it created quite a problem when Mary Hood died. Asa was already in his eighties when he married a third time to Victoria Harmon who was eighteen years old, but already had four children. Asa and his new family moved to Talladega, Alabama where a fifth child, John Ware, was born. According to my grandfather, Asa lost everything he owned in the Civil War. After the Civil War, there was not much left to divide up. Nevertheless at Asa's death there were considerable hard feelings among the three sets of children about the division of the properties that he had later acquired. The children of the second marriage were particularly unhappy because they, of necessity, had left home without anything. Litigation, it appears, went on for over a generation.

Shortly after the Civil War, Elisha who was thirteen, decided to leave home. He had very little education because the schools had been closed during the war. In a letter he wrote in October of 1924 he told my parents that the day he left home he was literally without a penny, and he walked all day until twilight looking for a job with a blacksmith. At that point in life being a blacksmith was his ideal vocation. He found three places that wanted a "striker," but was told in each place that he was too small. They told him he was not strong enough to handle the hammer. Not only was his pride deeply wounded, but he didn't have a cent to pay for a nights lodging. He walked on in the darkness until, as he said, "Darkness, Ghosts & Hobgoblins drove me to seek a place to spend the night." He wound up that "awful night" at the home of a Mr. A. C. Bennett. My grandfather wrote,

> I told Mr. Bennett my condition & said to him, 'I want to stay all night with you, but I have not one cent to pay for my lodging.' He said, 'My dear boy, I won't charge you one penny.' I said, 'Mr. Bennett I am much oblige to you, but I will not accept the proposition. We will talk the matter over in the morning.' Next morning I felt somewhat refreshed, but during the night, I thought over my plans for the next day. I got up in the night, wrote out a note for One Dollar to A.C. Bennett, or bearer, for this amount. The next morning, at the table, I had the note all prepared, & (Sic) handed it to him. He said, 'No, I won't charge you anything.' I told him <u>very</u> frankly, that I did not belong to the charity class. He finally said, 'I will accept the note, <u>because</u>, of your youth & manliness.' At

that time, I mean that night, something was said about prohibition, in which I expressed myself, unmistakably, a prohibitionist, Now this made a strong impression, on a young boy sitting close by, the <u>man</u>, & (sic) the Christian, that you know as Joe Bennett. Now about the note; 4 years later, I redeemed that note, & (sic) <u>no</u> paper, I ever possessed, lay closer to my heart than that(sic).

When my father grew up, Duluth was far removed from Atlanta. Most people made the trip by train. Duluth had a reputation in those days of having quite a number of illegal stills that made some mighty fine corn whisky. A story was told that once upon a time on a train going north from Atlanta the conductor went to sleep and was about to pass one of the stops without announcing the town. Someone waved a bottle of whisky under his nose and he woke up with a start and announced, "Doo Luth!" Another tale has it that a woman was buying a ticket for herself and her child at the ticket window in Atlanta, and she placed the money through the grated window telling the ticket agent, "Two to Duluth." To her surprise the ticket agent replied, "Twi-dill-lee-dee, Mam."

Lake Linear, which is west of the current city of Duluth, and is one of today's big attractions for Atlanta residence did not exist. The area around Duluth was hills and very thick woods with a few flat areas down by the river. The soil was not particularly good except to grown corn. But, people survived and for the most part the town flourished along the railroad tracks.

I had known that my grandfather was a physician, but I had not know until my Dad told me, that my grandfather had gone to Atlanta for two years for his training in medicine. At the time there were no medical schools as we know them today. It was a source of immense pride to him that he had actually studied medicine, and he insisted on being called Doctor Ware. People in Duluth who remember him or have heard about him still refer to him as Dr. Ware. I do not know what kind of practice he had; he was the only doctor in town. I gather that he treated almost everyone in town and the surrounding area. From what my father and uncle told me he was an avid reader and was well informed on both national and local events. His love and respect of learning was passed on to his children at a very early age.

When his children were still young he took them to Atlanta to the see the cyclorama of the Battle of Atlanta, although it had not been fully completed. The cyclorama is a life size reproduction of the Battle of Atlanta. A viewer passed under the set and came up through a stairwell on to a platform in the very middle of the battle. From the platform one viewed the battle in every direction with all of its gory details. The way in which the artist had built the work was such that the floor messed seamlessly into the walls. It gave the illusion of being able to see miles in every direction. Below the platform were life size sculptures of the soldiers, cannons, rifles, and animals. The battle then blended into the horizons of farmhouses and horseback riders. The artist had researched his work so well that the sculptures near the platform were recognizable persons who participate in the battle. The dead and wounded were replicas of actually fallen men. The cyclorama was a great work of art that still available to be seen in Atlanta, but at the time it was a grim reminder of the not too distant past. My father told me that there was a woman in their viewing group who recognized a member of her family and had to be led off the platform in tears. I can only guess the reasons for my grandfather taking the boys to the cyclorama, but I do know that he wanted his boys to grow up with an understanding of the world that was not limited to the hills and hollows of Gwinnett County, Georgia.

Even with three children my grandfather was a lonely man. I do not know why he never remarried. He was certainly young enough. My father once told me that at night he would occasionally find him crying, and when my dad would ask him what the problem was, it was always about missing my grandmother. It was not uncommon during this period of time for a man to outlast more than one wife. Child bearing and its dangers were all too natural for the period.

My grandfather was a very devout person, a leader in the Baptist Church for most of his adult life. He was a teetotaler. His strong prohibitionist views and actions got him into trouble more than one time with the local bootleggers in the hills around Duluth. He was forever telling the state revenuers where the illegal stills were hidden and often paid the consequence for passing on the information. Some times the farm animals were let out of their pastures or harassed, and other times it was more serious. The big barn back of the house was burned down by an irate moonshiner whose still had been found and destroyed because my grandfather had told the revenuers where it was located.

Living on the farm was often difficult. The boys did their share of the plowing and care of the livestock. It was hard manual labor. They knew years when the crops were good and years when the crops were bad. They even had the misfortune of having their smoke house burn down. Smokehouses in the area were build of logs which were raise above ground level in order to put slow burning hickory limbs under the floor so that the smoke could rise up through the floor and cure the meat. One had to be careful when curing hogs that the heat was not too great from the hickory limbs smoldering under the smokehouse. Unfortunately, one winter the hickory limbs were fanned by a light wind when the ventilator that controlled the burn under the house was not closed properly. The fat from the meat began to melt and dripped down through the cracks in the floor and before the night was over the smokehouse had burst into flame and all the pork was lost.

Actually my grandfather was both a physician and a farmer. Although my father attended school in Duluth, the farm was where he grew up. He never lost the love of farming even while we lived in China. Next to our home on the Baptist Compound in Shanghai, my dad always had a large garden. We also had at least one cow that grazed the campus grounds and provided the families at the Baptist Compound with milk, cottage cheese, and sometimes butter. The cow barn at the Compound was at the back of our house outside the high fence that enclosed the campus. I remember there being pigs, ducks, geese, and chickens out in the cow barn area. Immediately behind our house my father had planted grape vines, and every fall we had all the muscadines and scuppernongs we could eat and put up as preserves.

It seems that my Grandfather not only had horses, raise cows, and hogs, he even had goats. One of my uncle's favorite stories of their childhood was the time that a large billy goat climbed the hay stack in the barn and was up on the second floor of the building enjoying the hay and making a mess. The two boys who were about eight and ten years old were sent up the ladder to catch him and bring him down. The goat turned out to be ornery and loved to butt people who messed with him. In the hayloft he managed to elude them each time they were close to catching him. Finally they devised a strategy. Hawthorn would stand at the door of the hayloft through which the hay was loaded on to the second floor, and Hamilton, as my father was called by his family, would guide the goat toward the door. They almost had the goat cornered, when suddenly it lowered its head and charged Hawthorn in the open door. Luckily the goat's horns passed between his legs, but the goat's back raised him off the floor, out the door, through the air, and onto the barnyard below. He rode the goat all they way down and landed facing backwards, straddling the goat. All is well that ends well. No one was hurt. The goat was out of the hayloft, and Hawthorn had had the ride of his life.

I do not know when my father made a profession of faith and was baptized at the Duluth Baptist Church. My guess is that it was fairly early in their childhood that all three children made their professions of faith and were baptized. I do know that my father was very highly respected even when he was young by the members of the Baptist Church and the schoolteachers of Duluth schools. School classes were not carefully divided by age groups at the time, and it seems that my father, although two years younger than his older brother, was just as far along with his studies.

When they had gone as far as they could in the school in Duluth, my grandfather decided that it was time for them to go to college at the University of Georgia which was not too far way in Athens, Georgia. He did not think that it was wise to send Hawthorn there by himself. By this time Hawthorn had become a first rate baseball player and something of a ladies man. Hawthorn was seventeen and my Dad was fifteen when they applied to the University in 1908. They met with the Dean and after counting up all their credits they were each two credits short for admission. The Dean, being a rather pragmatic man, decided that they were actually qualified for the two credits that they lacked, and gave them two credits in Agriculture because they were raised on a farm. So my father went off to the University of Georgia at the age of fifteen to keep an eye on his older brother and keep him out of trouble. My Dad did well academically, and Hawthorn, though certainly no one's fool, became an outstanding baseball pitcher ready to enter the professional leagues.

It was in his first class at the University that my father decided to shorten his name. The class was taught by a rather awesome gentleman who enjoyed frightening young freshman. As each student would tell his name, the professor would comment, not so favorably, on the name with which each student identified them selves. My father full name was James Theodore Hamilton Carter Ware, far too long not to get a ridiculing comment from the professor. My father made a fast decision, and when his time came to speak up he identified himself as James

Hamilton Ware. It stuck. For the rest of his life he was James Hamilton Ware. He never used James. Often he used J. H. Ware. The people in Duluth knew him officially as Hamilton and those who knew him closely called him Hamp.

Hamp was not always able to keep his brother out of trouble. Hawthorne was handsome, somewhat reckless and a bit of a playboy; he really enjoyed the company of the girls in Athens. My Dad did well academically, and Hawthorn, though certainly no one's fool, became an outstanding baseball pitcher, ready to enter the professional leagues when he finished college. I think he played one summer with a farm team of one of the major leagues, but I have been unable to identify which one.

Hawthorn's dreams of the major leagues were over shadowed by a cute little red-head from Hogansville, Georgia, named Mary Edna Daniels. Aunt Mary, who was about five feet tall, was a lively, flirtatious person with lots of friends, and she was considered one of the most sought after women in Athens. The Daniels were relatively wealthy, leading citizens in Hogansville. Hawthorn and Mary made a hansom couple, athlete and society girl. They were married soon after graduation, and Hawthorn began his business career with Mary's help. I know that she worked with my uncle in his business as a secretary and bookkeeper, but I also think that Mary may have helped finance their start with Daniels' money. To say the least, she was indispensable in the early years of their business. Eventually they settled in Gastonia, North Carolina. where he opened Ware's Hardware store with the motto, "Ware's Hardware wears well."

My father's interests turned toward teaching. When he graduated, he had just past his nineteenth birthday, and was not ready to go into business, nor was he in a serious romance. Looking through a box of old family papers that my younger sister had kept, I found several telling recommendation written both by prominent merchants and teachers in Duluth and the University of Georgia. My father began collecting recommendations in September of 1912. Mr. J.W. Knox and his partners T.A. Lewis, C.A. Summerour, and J. H. Summerour, wrote a letter of recommendation on their general merchandise company stationary, Knox, Lewis & Company, that read:

> We have known Hamilton Ware all his life and have never know of his doing any thing of a low or degrading nature. He was always considered a good boy while in school and is now one of our best young men. He was a bright pupil while in school always standing high in his classes- He has had fine opportunities since he left here – Has always connected himself with Church and Sunday School. Think he will make a good teacher should he make that his profession. He will do his best at whatever he undertakes.

Mr. C.O. Maddox, the Cashier for the Farmers and Merchants Bank, wrote: ". . . I have known Mr. Hamilton Ware for some time and feel free, and am glad to give him a letter of recommendation. He is a man of high character, and is competent to fill the position he is seeking." W.F. Harney, one of his teachers in Duluth who had moved way to Smyrna, Georgia, stated that Mr. Hamilton Ware had been his student in 1907-1908 in Duluth, and, he had. . . "found him to be a conscientious, pains-taking student, thorough in his studies, and a gentleman in every respect." The Principal of Duluth High School, Mr. Robert R. Buckley, was equally high in his praise. He wrote, "I have known Mr. Ware for some time and have found his character, reputation, and training to be of exceptionally high standard. In a few words, if you want a good sound practical man for a position of great responsibility you will make no mistake in selecting Mr. Ware." Hamp's English Professor at the University of Georgia, Prof. R. E. Park, wrote: "It is with great pleasure that I endorse Mr. J.H. Ware for the position as teacher in the public school system of the State. Mr. Ware is capable of handling any of the branches taught in the high school, as he is a thorough student, and a man of great ability. He is of the highest character, conscientious and upright."

It seems that my father began teaching that fall at Fincherville School near Mc Dougal, Georgia, although he had not gotten a teaching certificate. It was not an easy year and the school building was in seriously bad repair. On May 15, 1913 he received a letter from Mr. K.H. Mattox the Secretary- Treasurer of the patrons of the Fincherville School asking him to please return for the 1913 school year. They promised him that they would level and re-floor the present building and add a 30 X 40 room. They also agree to paint the inside and the outside of the building and to fix the well. The house would be in an "up-to-date shape." The Masons in the community would build a second story to the house for their meeting place, a guarantee that the building would be well cared for. Please, wouldn't he consider returning to Fincherville?

Four days after his twentieth birthday, Hamilton went to Jackson, Georgia and took the State of Georgia's examination for High School teachers, and on July 29th he received notice from Mr. C.S. Maddox the Superintendent of the County Board Of Education of Butts County, that he had not only done well, but that the paper which he submitted was excellent. Now he officially had a First Grade license to teach in the Public Schools of Georgia. He had taken the tests in Mathematics, English, and Science and had averaged a 95 8/9 average score. His highest scores were in math.

My Dad did not return to Fincherville, but decided to use the summer to strengthen his credentials. He enrolled at the University of Tennessee in Knoxville and took courses in Adolescence, Oriental and Greek History, The Essentials of Composition, Roman History and Plant Life. During the summer he received an invitation to teach in the southern part of the state at Shellman, at what was then known as Shellman Institute and later as Shellman High School. He was to stay in Shellman the rest of his public school teaching years.

Although there is some indication that Hamilton looked for other teaching positions after his first year at Shellman Institute, he stayed there until the spring of 1916. In the spring of 1914, after his first year, I. A. Martin, Chairman of the Board of Trustees of Shellman Institute wrote: "Mr. J. H. Ware has been the a member of the faculty here the past school year & has proved himself well prepared for the work undertaken. He has given intense satisfaction & I regret to see him leave realizing that his place will be hard to fill. He has had practically no trouble in discipline &

is a good instructor. Quiet and orderly in His behavior of good moral character & perfect gentleman (sic)." What Mr. Martin did not know, or at least what he did not say, was that Hamilton made close friends with his students. One of his ex-students told me that he was not above walking on his hands in class to illustrate a point. I gather that he was not above clowning around while he was teaching. Although he was not as athletic as Hawthorn, my father was always in good physical shape and enjoyed physical activities. It was not unusual for him to play baseball, basketball and other sports with his students. Most of his students were five, six, or seven years younger than he was, but several of them kept in touch with him after he left Shellman. I have a picture of him with the Principal, J.W. Davis, and twelve members of his ninth grade class. One of the young women in the picture was Jessie Lee Bell. Jessie would correspond occasionally with my father over the entire time that he was on the mission field. My father got to know the entire Bell family well. Several years after my mother's death, Jessie read in the *Commission,* a publication of the Southern Baptist Foreign Mission Board, that my father had gone to Hong Kong for a year as the pastor of the Kowloon Baptist Church. Upon his return to the United States, he received a letter from Jessie, who was living in Franklin, North Carolina. Her husband had died a number of years earlier and she was teaching school in Franklin, A romance developed. But I am getting far ahead of the story.

In the summer of 1915 Hamp did not stay in Shellman, but went to the University of Virginia in Charlottesville, and took two English courses toward a Masters Degree. I had always known that my father was good in math and science, but I did not know of his interest in literature until I began researching through his old papers. He seems to have greatly enjoyed both the course in Shakespeare and a course in Tennyson and Browning. I don't think he ever taught either of these courses in the years that followed.

At the end of the school year in 1916 my Dad decided to leave Shellman. For his colleagues and students it was like a death in the family. J.W. Davis wrote:

> My feelings were too near the surface today for me to say anything about what a pleasure and benefit it has been to me to have been associated with you for the past two years both in and out of the schoolroom. You have, without an exception, been big enough to look over all of my petty ideas and mistakes and I am truly appreciative and it is my desire that in the future I shall have an opportunity of showing just what my appreciation is.

At the end of his letter he adds: "With every good wish to you for your speedy recovery, I am most truly, J.W. Davis. Let me hear from you."

I do not have any idea what my father's illness was, but it does not seem to have been extensive. In 1917 he attended Atlanta Business College, but I do not think that he was in a degree program. My uncle Hawthorn mentioned to me on one occasion that my father had sold insurance before he went to seminary. If he did it was during 1917. His public school teaching career was over, although he had an invitation to teach in the Madison Public School system in the fall of 1916; and, as late as August of 1919 an offer to teach in Stark High School for seven month at the large sum of $25.00 a month. Although President Wilson had declared neutrality two years earlier, in the spring of 1917 it appeared that war with Germany was inevitable. But my father was trying to decide what his life was going to be and how he might serve God. By the spring and summer of 1917 he had come to the conclusion that he should be in training for the ministry. I do not know the details of his sense of calling, but in the years to come he never looked back. My sense and the sense of other who have known him was that he thoroughly embraced his work as God's calling, although his particular assignments were always changing. In the fall of 1917, although the War had begun for the United States, Hamilton entered Southern Baptist Theological Seminary in Louisville, Kentucky. But at the end of the spring term of the next year, like so many young men, my father enlisted in the military. In those days your dog tag not only gave your birth date, but also the date of your enlistment. I found my father dog tag in an old steel cash box that has been hidden away for years on a closet shelf. He joined the Navy on May 31, 1918. It seems that he chose the Navy expecting to travel and see the world, but wound up on a minesweeper in South Carolina's Charleston harbor. My father never talked to me about his few months in the Navy. It was not that he was anti-military, he was proud to have served his country during World War I. There were very few times when I saw my father cry, but while we were living in Staunton, Virginia he visited us. One afternoon he was watching a documentary on World War I, and from behind Him I could see his shoulders shaking as he relived the War.

The experience in Charleston seems to have been boring. On one occasion he told my sister that the meanest man he had ever met had been his boot-camp instructor. As part of their training they were made to stand on a sandy beach while insects bit their legs. No one was to complain; this was part of learning how to live with hardships. I do not know when my father got out of the Navy, but he was back in Louisville at the Southern Baptist Theological Seminary by the fall of 1919 pursuing a master's degree in Theology. While Wilson was pushing for a just peace and the formation of the League of Nations, Hamilton was in the classes of A. T. Robertson, W. O. Carver, E.Y. Mullins, and William Hersey Davis, some of the best scholars ever produced by Southern Baptist.

In his senior year he was ordained by the Ninth and O Street Baptist Church, even though he had not yet had a call to a pastorate. It was also in his senior year that he met Mary Bibb Long, one of the young women at the Women's Missionary Training School in Louisville. My father's interest in missions was not as focused as my mother's. At one time he thought about going into mountain work. By the end of the year he had decided to go to the mission field, and he volunteered to go wherever he would be needed the most. I think he thought at the time that this might be Africa. As far as I can determine his acquaintance with Mary Bibb at this time was not a serious relationship; it certainly was not for her. They may have gone places together with groups of other students, but I don't think they ever spent much time with one another in Louisville.

After graduation from seminary the candidates for the mission field went to Richmond, Virginia to meet with members of the Foreign Mission Board and to be formally appointed to their respective fields. It was already clear that Hamilton would be going to the mission field in North China to undertake a new type of mission work for Southern Baptist that was very much like that being done by the Y.M.C.A.. His institutional work would be with young Chinese men and women. This was confirmed at the Mission Board Meeting with his formal appointment to North China. It seems that my father and mother traveled on the same train from Richmond to their respective homes and shared with each other some of their concerns. They came to know each other somewhat better than they had in seminary. My mother discussed with him her father's reluctance to let her go to China. When they got to Atlanta, Hawthorn, my father's brother, met them at the train to take Hamilton home. Mother saw Hamp there, but later told Mer, the name my Grandmother used to sign her letters to her daughter, that he seemed to be a nice person, but that she really did not have time to talk with him.

During the summer Hamilton made his home with his brother Hawthorn and his wife Mary in Winder, Georgia. It seems that my Grandfather was also there for most of the summer, having retired from his practice in Duluth. Hamilton was in an out all summer long preaching at small revivals and meetings.

Not long after they had gotten home Hamilton began writing to Mary Bibb. She seems not to have answered his first two letters. When she got the third letter from him she wrote back addressing Hamilton as, "Dear Sir." Not willing to be outdone, he wrote back, "'Dear Madam,' They tell me that is the proper way to reply to a 'Dear Sir.' You didn't know I could be so particular, did you? Down right mean would be a better way to describe me." In fact for several months Bibb referred to Hamilton as Mr. Ware with her friends and family although he signed his letters Hamp. She kept the relationship very proper.

It was a busy summer for Hamp. In June he had two "meetings," one for ten days and the second for eight days in which he preached both morning and evening services. It had been two years since he had done this sort of work, and he was very gratified with it. Unfortunately his mail was not forwarded to him (some of the letters had been returned to sender) and he did not receive my Mother's letters until he got back to Winder. In her later letters she included the one's which had been returned to her. It seems that she shared with him that her father's attitude toward her going to China was somewhat changing. He replied, "My people are not opposing me – they are not enthusiastic though over my going. They seem unhappy and can't see why I should remain longer than seven years. I ought to make an exception of my sister who has been very pleasant about it all along."

My father was planning a full summer of church work before he left for China. He already had his passport, and hoped that Bibb too was ready to go and had nothing to do but ". . . let people 'Love the Missionary.' It must be fine to find out that people love a preacher sometimes. One little girl about eight actually cried the other day when I told her good bye." One other plan he had for the summer before he left the United States. was to get a front tooth that was broken off fixed. His dentist had never made an enamel tooth, but promised him that he would not let him look like a "gold brick." The dentist did a fine job. Although my Father never gave a toothy smile for his pictures, I never knew he had ever had a broken tooth.

On August the sixteenth Hamp wrote that he was finishing up his summer work with "Dock" Bone, a young seminary friend who had been called as pastor to several rural churches in Georgia. He had preached the first two nights of a revival for his friend, and had only one more meeting before he would leave for the West Coast. He was cutting it close because he was to leave Georgia the twenty-first for Cincinnati, Chicago, and Seattle. Unlike my mother, my father chose to slip off from Winder in order not to cause a scene with the neighbors. I think that he had hoped to travel from Chicago to Seattle on the same train as my mother, but there is no indication that they made connections or that they were with each other until the S.S. Hawkeye sailed from Seattle. He was still signing his letters, Sincerely, Hamp Ware.

Hamp and Mary Bibb must have spent more than a little time together on the Hawkeye. The tone of his letters to her changed dramatically after she left him in Kobe to go on to Shanghai. From Kobe he wrote her that she was all he could think about. "For an old bachelor" it all seemed so bemusing. "Say," he writes, "you don't suppose I am going crazy, do you?" If they had to send him to an asylum, he would go happy. He was very taken back by mother's frankness in discussing her ideals and desires, and found himself listening to them in joy and approval. "I can't see, to save me, how you have been able to trust yourself to me as you have." No one had ever opened themselves up to my father like my mother did, and he vowed to take it as a sacred trust, even her chiding. She had spoken to him about being too humble; to which he replied, ". . . I really feel very humble right now in the sight of our Father for His good hand that has always blessed me beyond my understanding." Things were very different for both of them. Several times later in letters my father mentioned his memories of the last night on the Hawkeye. I think that on that last night he had proposed to her and gotten a tentative, yes. Mother had to consult with her family before the final commitment. Hamp's letter from Kobe was signed, "With love, Jim"

A second letter sent from Kobe, Japan to Shanghai on September the thirteenth tells of his shopping spree with the four missionary ladies that got off the boat there with him. But the majority of the letter focuses on a picture of herself that my mother gave him. He was truly head over heels in love. This letter was signed, "With a heart full of love, Jim" Two days later he would be on his way to Tsingtao, China on board a Japanese freighter of the Osaka Shosen Kaisha Line, the S.S. Taiboku Maru.

My father's arrival in China was entirely different from my mother's, although they crossed the pacific together on the S.S. Hawkeye. Almost forty years later in 1960 my sister made my father sit down and record the events that occurred on his arrival in China. In his words:

> Really my experience as a missionary began in Japan. We were traveling out to the Orient, a group of new missionaries some fifty or sixty, and of that number there were four of us, two single ladies (Miss Bennett and Miss Grayson) and

two single men (my self and Robert Pruit), who were going to what was called our North China Mission which was located in Shandong Province of China. The two single men were. . . one was the son of a missionary family who had finished his college work and was going back to China to help his father in college, and he was blind. The other young man was me. We had with us a young missionary by the name of Miss Smith (Bertha Smith), who had been home on her first furlough after her first term of service. She was from North China also. So, naturally she took charge of us four young missionaries because we did not know where to turn or what to do. I found out later that she changed the usual plan of doing things. Usually, we would stay on the ocean liner until we reached the big city of Shanghai and then we would transfer to a coastal boat up to Shandong and North China. But for some reason Miss Smith decided that it was best for us to get off in Japan and take a Japanese freighter across to Tsingtao which was one of the port for entry in North China. So when Miss Smith told us to get off in Japan. We got off like Miss Smith told us to do. I took, of course, the blind man in hand because I was the only other man in the group. We got off ship and got our baggage in Kobe, Japan; headed out for the one hotel in Kobe where they were prepared to take care of foreigners. This was early in September. When we arrived at the hotel we found out that they had only one room available. And so you can imagine with three single ladies and two single men who got the room at the hotel. Well. Miss Smith arranged for us to go to a Japanese hotel. No one there spoke English, and they were not use to caring for foreign guest. So they took care of us like they thought foreigners ought to be care for, and they cooked food for us like they thought foreigners ought to eat. We had about five days, nearly a week, there in Kobe before this Japanese freighter pulled out. So, we had about five days in the Japanese hotel where the Japanese idea how foreign food ought to be cooked. (sic) Then we got on the Japanese freighter; and, as you know, freighters have only a limited passage for passengers, and it happened that we five seemed to be the only passenger on the freighter going across the Yellow Sea to Tsingtao. There again, no one on the ship spoke English, and Miss Smith didn't speak Japanese. So, we were cared for by the cook on a Japanese freighter like he thought foreigners ought to be cared for. Well, by the time we made it across the Yellow Sea, which took us about, I think, three days, something like that, to get across, we landed in Tsingtao late in the afternoon (sic). One of our older missionaries met us at the ship, Dr. Morgan. The first thing that he said to us was, 'well I'm sorry we have only one missionary house in Tsingtao, and we have just one guest room in our home. So, you can imagine who got the guestroom, three single ladies and two young men. And he said, 'I have arranged for the two young men to go to a hotel.'

Tsingtao was build, if you remember, by the Germans. A nice little port, (sic) had been taken over right at the end of World War One; had been taken over during World War I by the Japanese, and they were still in control of that Japanese peninsular at that time, and had not turned it back to the Chinese (sic). Rather they're(sic) quite a summer resort up north, so the hotel were still pretty well filled when we arrived there along about the middle of September. And he said, I have arranged for you a hotel; so we thought, well a hotel it would be. He took us to a hotel and turned us over to the people at the hotel, did not stop to see what arrangements were made for us (sic). I had never been in China and did not know anything about it. Robert couldn't see, the blind man; and he had been away since he was a boy. And, I doubt if he knew much about it. So finally they took us out across the lawn to the wall, to some rooms that were made along the wall not in the main building of the hotel (sic). I found out later after I had lived in China for a while that these rooms, out along the wall, were built originally, and always for servants. And apparently they used these rooms for over flow rooms for guests during the summer crowding season. Well, the man in the hotel turned us over to a Chinese boy who spoke Pidgin English. He couldn't speak good English. And, when he carried us in to this little room; I saw one single bed in the room, and call his attention, 'just one bed,' and he said, 'By by will come.' So, I thought that if he said, 'By by will come,' then by by it would come. I did not bother about it. It was near suppertime; getting dark by then. So I led Robert across the lawn to the main hotel. When we went into the dinning room to get our supper, I found out that it was an English hotel, not an American. So our food for the evening was what the Englishmen considered as a right supper for an Englishman to eat. So with our English supper, and since we were all pretty tired after that trip across the Yellow Sea, we headed back for our room. When I got right up back to our room, I found in one corner of the room a little, what you call a love seat, or something like that, you know the old timers with a lot of curly cues to it. And, you could get two people on it, if by crowding them, I know (sic); and several blankets laying up on it. It was getting along the later part of September; it was cold up there in North China. So, I thought, well, he said. 'by by will come'; this is it. Of course I put the blind boy on the bed. And, then I tried to sleep on that little love nest. I had my neck up on one end for a while and had my feet hanging off, and put my feet up for a while and hung my neck off. So my first night in China proper was like that. After an English idea of breakfast, Dr. Morgan came in and took us in his car, and took us on sightseeing trip around Tsingtao; it was right after the war, showing us where the big battle had been fought, the Japanese and the Germans, and so forth (sic). We ended at his home shortly before dinner. When we sat down at his table for dinner, it was the first American meal I had seen in about ten days. And I was really ready to sit down and eat something that I was use to eating. And I really enjoyed that first meal I had in a missionary home. Well, hadn't been in the home very long before dinner another older missionary had come in, and I saw him and Dr. Morgan head off privately into Mr. Morgan's office. And I could hear a conversation going on in there. I didn't know what it was all about, but I learned later on what all the conversation was about in that office when I got to the first mission station. Dr. Sears was from that station. And they were arranging for our arrival at the first mission station. So, we hadn't finished dinner very long when Dr. Morgan said it was time for us to get down to the train 'You know the Japanese don't wait for you. If you don't get on they don't bother.' We got the tickets; and, 'if you don't get off they don't bother.' (sic) They are on the train and put off the baggage (sic). Passengers, they take their tickets up at the railroad station, and that's it. So, if you want a good seat you'll have to get down there. So, we head out to the railroad station. I guess it was along about four o'clock when our train pulled out for the interior of China, run by the Japanese. Well, it was well after dark when we reached the station where we were going to get off for the night. When we got near to that station, Bertha Smith began to tell us, 'Now, what he said is so. Japanese are just going to stop this train at Wei Shin just long enough to put off any baggage and tend to any business, and they are going right on whether we get off or not; it doesn't make any difference.' Well, you can imagine three young single ladies going to China for at least six or seven years, how many pieces of small baggage we had. We had to keep account of it by counting it. I think we had twenty-four small pieces of baggage that had to be unloaded. We decided that if we go those twenty-four pieces of small baggage off and our crowd off, we were going to have to organize a little bit. So one of the single ladies agreed to get the blind man off and two of the single ladies were going to hop off as soon as soon as the train stopped, and I was to pull up the window. And we had it open when they arrived. I would pull baggage and shoot it through the window and they would take it out. And, if any one got left on the train, I would be the one left on the train. So, we arrived and sure enough we didn't have much time. The two single ladies got outside, and I began to shoot the baggage. About the time I was beginning to get the last two or three pieces through the window the train began to move. So by the time I got to the steps and got off a shan tse. And: a shan tse is made by taking two long poles about four inches in diameter and in the center of them they place some cross pieces to hole them apart. Then they pulled netting over that area in the center. Then, put a covered wagon sort of a thing over the top of that (sic). In the front end between the poles you put a mule and in the hind in between the poles you put a mule. And they have a kind of wooden saddle that goes up on the back of each mule and the wooden poles fit into that saddle on the back of the mules. And, that was called the Shandong Pullman. You could sit down in it if you wanted to sit and dangle you legs out behind the mule in front, or you could lie down if you had enough pillows and cover to lie down with. According to ordinary travel, one man one shan tse, that's the way we usually traveled; one man one shan tse. And the people at the first mission station were supposed to have sent us five shan tse, one for each person. And, each shan tse carried enough bedding for each person. And only one shan tse had arrived. Well, she became very much worried. Well, they said, 'The man is here and you can talk to him.' He said one more shan tse might come, but he wouldn't get here tonight. He might meet us on the road. But it is planting time and the fall of the year and the mules are all busy in the fields, and they just couldn't get the shan tses. And we had just one shan tse and enough bedding for one person. Well, after we finished our supper. . . 'enough bedding for one person'(sic). I don't need to tell you who got the bedding. Miss Smith called the innkeeper and told him to take us to our place to spend the night. I didn't know where it would be. He took his little Japanese type lantern, that you know, with a little pole stick holding it up and a candle inside a paper lantern. He started across the courtyard inside the inn, a big that courtyard to the guest room and the girls had prepared our canned breakfast the next morning. After breakfast we started out, one shan tse, five people. I can see it now. I couldn't see it at night. I could see the enclosure and see the animals and see all the rest just as the sun came up. We started up a little hill on our trail to the first mission station which would be thirty-five miles away. And we had to cover that day to the first mission station (sic). I can see that first sunrise that I saw in China to this moment. As we started up that little hill, the sun came up. Well, we started out with three single ladies, a blind man, and my self and one shan tse. Now you can imagine what chances I had of getting any ride. It just wasn't any use in talking about me riding. Those girls hadn't walked but a mile or two and they began to give out. So, they began to beg the shan tse man to let two ride. And, finally they (I don't know whether Miss Smith used some money or what), but they finally got consent for two to ride at a time. So, they got to riding two at a time, and they would take turns. Well that left me, of course, to continue to walk. The blind man and one of the girls would take a turn, and then the other two girls would take a turn riding. Along about ten or eleven o'clock in the morning we came to a large river. They had a ferry, an old time ferry, to cross the river. And, as we were waiting there for the ferry to come across, some body looked over on the other side and said, 'I believe I see another shan tse over there. I wonder if that shan tse is going to meet us?' Well, they were getting pretty tired by that time; already had three or four hours of it (sic). Ah, when we crossed over, sure enough it was the second shan tse. So, we had two shan tse from then on. But, the mules from the first one were already tired, and the folks were already tired; so there wasn't any use talking about me riding any that day.

About the only real experience I remember during the walk that day was, ah, we came to a wide sort of a mud hole proposition (sic). It was, I guess, about fifteen or twenty feet wide. The water was about, not quite, knee deep in it. Miss Smith said, 'Now I'll show you young missionaries how to ride across a thing like this.' And, we were learning our first lesson, and she called one of the coolies and had him to bend over, put his hand back of himself like that, and then she put her knees in his hands and leaned over on his back. Well, it was a time when they had these hobbled skirts. Miss Smith's feet stuck up like a duck. I can see those feet to this day sticking up like a duck on its back. Sticking up like that, I looked at that, and I said, 'That may be the way you do it, but I'm not going to be caught doing that, going to ride a coolie's back. I'll walk a mile before I'll do it.' So I set off trying to find out some way to get around that thing. Well, I don't know how far I walked, but I managed to get around without riding the coolies back. By the time I got back they had all gotten across and headed down the road. That was the only outstanding event of that day. We arrived in Ping Tu, our first mission station, thirty-five miles for the day, about nine o'clock at night. We left at sun up that morning and arrived there about nine o'clock that night. Then I had my first experience in a mission home; found out what Dr. Morgan and Dr. Sears were arguing about back there in that room. You see it so turned out that all the men in the Ping Tu station happened to be away at that time. There wasn't a single person at the station except women. According to Chinese custom men (are) just not supposed to stay in a house where there are ladies without another man in the house. And, they did not what us to ruin our reputation, and we were just there; and they had tried to figure out back there in Tsingtao how they were going to work that proposition. So, they had wired ahead to tell Mrs. Sears, who was an Australian, by the way, married to an American, Dr. Sears' wife (sic). They had wired ahead and told her how to arrange the things. They were to put us in the doctor's house, and he wasn't there at all, so that would be an empty house; and that wouldn't give any trouble. And the single ladies they knew how to take care of. Well, we walked up to one of these missionary houses and knocked on the door, and a lady came to the door and opened that door and saw us two men standing there, the blind man and me. She started out with a loud voice, 'Come right in. Come into my house. You will spend the night right here. Anyone tell me how to run my house (sic). Come right in young men; come right in. No one is going to tell me how to run my business. Well, she told us to come in, and I was ready to come in by nine o'clock at night; so I went in. And we spent the night that night in Mrs. Sears house with Dr. Sears not being there. Well, the women in the station were terribly concerned when they found out I had not had a single ride all day and had had to walk thirty- five miles in my first real day in China. They were very much concerned about that. So, they couldn't get a shan tse still, but they were determined that I shouldn't have to do that the next day (sic). So, they began to figure out something about it. And the next morning when they said, 'You have to move out rather early. It is about twenty-five miles to the next station, and it will take nearly all day to make it. So, we would like you to take time to visit, but don't have time (sic). So, we will have to send you out.' So, early after breakfast they took us out to send us on our way. What I found out was, when I got out to get on a shan tse, I didn't have a shan tse. What I had was one of these little Chinese donkeys which is about, oh, I guess, a little higher than my chest. I could sit on him and almost dangle my feet on the ground. And they had prepared the donkey for me to ride. They couldn't get a shan tse; they got a couple of shan tses for the others, but they got a donkey for me. And the way they had a saddle on the donkey was, they just had a pile of old cloths thrown across his back and then a great big piece of cloth over the top of those cloths and tied around the animal as tight as they could tie it. And that was my saddle. Remember now, it was a good size Chinese city, and I crawled up there. They insisted that I get on the donkey and start riding. I crawled up on that donkey and reached for the reins. A little boy, about I reckon, thirteen or fourteen years old, the donkey belonged to him, and he shook his head. 'No'. He wasn't going to let me have the reins. He was going to see that I didn't run that donkey or mistreat him. He was going along, going to lead that donkey all the way with me sitting up there on it. So you can see what the situation was; I was leading the parade. Sitting on top of a donkey, just as big as the donkey was, my feet dangling down to the ground, a little Chinese boy leading the donkey, and here were these other foreigners in two shan tse coming along behind me down the main street of this city. Well, if anybody felt like a fool, I sure did. That was one time I was sure I was on parade, because they did see too many foreigners around, and a foreigner riding on this little donkey was something to see. But I had plenty of viewers as I rode through the city down the main street to the city wall and out. As soon as I could I got off the donkey, I decided I had rather walk than be a showpiece like that. I just didn't like the gate of the donkey anyhow. So, I didn't ride the donkey very much, so the little boy got very much disgusted with me, so that when dinnertime came we stopped in a little, good size Chinese town. The boy announced to Miss Smith that he was going back home and taking his donkey home. So, about half way to the next town he turned back and left me to hoof it the rest of the way. Then we made it into the next place called Lei Chou Fu. I guess we better not do much more than that. When we got to Lei Chou Fu though, one of the single ladies and Miss Smith were to stop there. That was their station. So that left one single lady, the blind man and myself to go on to the next station which was two days trip. We found out when we got there that each one of us three who were to go on to the next station had somebody to come meet us. The single lady had a single lady to meet her. I had a young single man, a doctor's son who had returned to China, met me. Robert Pruitt, the blind man's father had come to meet him. Well, they said to us, 'It a shame to put these new missionaries like this, just rush them through. Why don't we just let them see something as they go.' We don't know when they will get back through here and get to see this. Good thing they did because I never got back. And they asked us, the single women and me, if we would like to spend a day and get a little rest. Well, I said, 'Yes, I'd be glad to rest a day. And I'd be glad to see a little of the mission as I went through.' Well, we didn't know that we and the scenic islands of the Inland Sea. He says that he is getting a bit "mushy" and "gushy." He probably was since the group he was with had begun to tease him a bit about Bibb. They wanted him to describe her in "Lover's English." He must have embellished his accounts because he says that he didn't think they believed letter she had presupposed that Hamp had done the same thing.

On his trip to Hwangshin Hamp wrote one more letter under his pseudonym "Jim" and mailed it from Lai Chou on the twenty second of September. In the letter he recalled many of the experiences that he later recorded on the tape for my sister. On Sunday they had been in Pingtu and went to church where they were welcomed by the Chinese congregation and then given a formal reception by the missionaries there. Mr. Leonard, one of the missionaries, took him up on one of the mountains near Pingtu where you could see "a thousand villages" on a clear day. "What a field to labor in!" he wrote. The children in Pingtu with their bright eyes especially appealed to him. Most of them, he noted, were part of a large colony of orphans from a distant district that had undergone a sever drought. "I know your heart would go out to them." signed, "With Love, Jim."

Hamp reached Hwangshin on September twenty-fifty, and there was a letter there for him from Bibb. It was the next day before he replied; she must have included the letter that she had written to Dr. Ray. Both of them were now in China where they had been appointed. Both had been received with open arms and challenged with the work which lay ahead of them. Both of them had written Dr. Ray. What had been a solemn agreement on the decks of the S.S. Hawkeye, that either one of them would transfer from their field to be with the other, would now face the test of reality, the wishes of the Foreign Mission Board, and the wishes of their fellow missionaries.

CHAPTER TWO

Mary Bibb

Mother went to China in 1921 to spread the Christian gospel and emancipate Chinese women. It turned out to be a much more difficult assignment than she had anticipated. Once she was committed to going, no one was able to dissuade her. She went explicitly against the wishes of her father, "Judge" Long, who threaten to disinherit her if she left home to live in China halfway around the world. On January twenty seventh 1921, before her graduation from the Women's Missionary Union Training School in Louisville, Kentucky, she wrote to her Papa:

> You may say I speak like a crazy person and that if it weren't for your help I'd be teaching, the last is true in a measure, but I believe if I didn't have you, Papa, to give me my support God would raise up others that I might carry out His plan in my life. I'm glad that the Holy Spirit has taught me to trust thus and glad that the same promises I have are yours if you will accept them. You will be

happier, home will be home, and all will be better, Papa. . . .

Dr. Ray, the Foreign Miss. Sec. has been to see us and I'm reasonably sure that I'll be appointed in June to sail in August, the dream of fourteen years is going to be realized at last. It is not easy to go and leave home and the dear ones, but unless there's some real reason for my not going which God does not remove, I could not be happy in America even surrounded with plenty, friends, and all that people generally enjoy. I do not want you and Mer to grieve over my going or feel I'm burying my life. I'm not. I'm just going on a long love journey as an ambassador, a volunteer for Him. You'll be glad I did when we stand around the great white throne and I can say, 'I went where you wanted me to go, I did what you wanted me to do.' I want you to find joy in my going.

She was his oldest daughter. There was a special bond between them that one often finds between a father and his oldest daughter. Even though he had earlier told her that he was willing to pay her salary as a missionary, only when he realized on the week before she left that she was truly going, did he give his reluctant consent for her to go to China. There were four other children in the family, but none of them made the "Judge" more proud. Although she and her father did not always see eye to eye, the depth of her love for him was deep and tender. In their adult life her two brothers were for periods of time partners with their father in his law practice. She never had that type of close working relationship; rather, it was an understood relationship of intimacy.

Among the many papers I had boxed up from the old home place when it was finally sold, I found a three page, single typed note titled, "A Sketch of Mary Bibb Ware in the Foreign Mission Field," written "by a doting Mother". In it my grandmother stated:

> Her father, and I, at first thought, that with maturing years the idea of being a foreign missionary would probably give way. But not so as it grew with her maturity and strengthened her will for that end.

> At no time did Mary Bibb allow any of the usual allurements swerve her from faith in the goal she had set.

> As time passed, this became a serious matter with her parents. The father was hopeful the idea would fade, and I began to wonder, "How much of my teaching to the Sunbeams I had really meant." I had not thought of one of my girls going to China. I had done my work better than I "Dreamed."

Both of her parents were born during the period immediately after the Civil War, and their upbringing evolved out of Southern culture and Southern family life. Family was the only safe haven in the society, and family ties and loyalties, family lore and records were passed on from generation to generation. To trace one's family history from the American Colonial period to the American Civil

War takes a long time and a great deal of patience. Julia Miller Dean, Bibb's sister did the pains taking job, and for her efforts became a member of the DAR, Daughters of the American Revolution. I think that she trace the family history through the Camfield line. For their immediate history, however, occasionally something was written down on a sheet of paper or recorded in a dairy and put away in a cardboard box in the back of a closet, but for the most part it was shared at family gatherings or visits to the family graveyards. My grandmother and my mother saved many of the letters that they wrote to one another from 1916 to 1961, the year of my mother's death. I found a scrapbook that my Grandmother kept of letters and memorabilia that mother saved from her initial trip to China and the first several months thereafter. The content of those letters sometimes became part of the family lore; however, I was not aware of some of the more personal things that were mentioned in them until I began sorting and reading the letters.

As a child, I heard the stories and visited the tombstones of both of my parent's ancestors and kin. After Sunday lunch when the plates had been cleared from the huge oval oak table in the dinning room, we would listen while someone told the tales that we had heard time and time again. Sometimes there were as many as four generations around the table all wrapped in the memories, the story telling, of the family exploits, antecdotes, and memorable events of the past. Mother was a product of two post Civil War southern families bound together by her parent's marriage, and the stories which they told one another about their pasts.

Tupelo, Mississippi has had more than its share of crusaders and its famous people. Mary Bibb was one of those during the early twentieth century. She was named Mary for her grandmother Mary Catherine Edwards Long and Bibb for her grandmother Augusta Bibb Campfield Holden. Bibb was a Holden family name through the marriage of a Freeman cousin into the Bibb family. The Bibbs were prominent during the period in Georgia history. One of the Bibb clan was a governor of Georgia and another was a Confederate general. For much of mother's life she was known by her middle name, Bibb. On formal occasions it was Mary Bibb or Miss Mary Bibb, but for the most part her family and her friends simply called her Bibb.

From the beginning Mother seemed destined to carry on the tradition of her namesake and paternal grandmother, Mary Catherine Edwards, one of Samuel C. Edwards and Zelphia Hill's five children. She was born in Mecklenburg County, North Carolina, on. March 25, 1836. Her family moved to Pulaski, Tennessee when she was fairly young and stayed there for several years before moving to Palmetto, Mississippi where they built their home and farmed about a mile and a half south of the Palmetto Methodist Church. Mr. Sam McCord married the oldest of Mary's three sisters. When the first sister died, he married a second sister, who also died young. Mr. Mc Cord then married a third Edwards sister. When Mc Cord died, Mary married William Bodenheimer Long in 1860 before he served in the Civil War as a Captain in the 41st Mississippi Regiment.

During the Civil War, Mary's only brother, Samuel, was killed in the battle of Perryville, Kentucky. Mr. Mc

Cord also fought in the Civil War and lost an arm in the fighting. Numerous small and medium size engagements between the Union armies and the Confederates took place in North Mississippi during the Civil War. Mary was a small gutsy redhead and ran the Union blockade in a horse and buggy in order to get medical supplies to the Confederate soldiers in Palmetto after the battle of Harrisburg just west of Tupelo.

Palmetto sent many other young men to war. John Marshall, and Winslow Garmon, Captain William Cunningham, Addison Davis, Mitchell Malone, Dow Howell, William Kirkpatrick, my great grandfather Captain W. B. Long and his brother Lieutenant P.S. Long, Thomas Freeman, Bill Hamilton, Burt Donavan, Jim Long and his brother Dan (no direct kinship with our Long family) all served in the Confederate Army. The story is told that Tobe McPherson, another Palmetto boy, volunteered with four other young men to bring in a sack of Federal colors flying from the rail pile in front of the breastworks at Fredericksburg, Virginia. They found on reaching the objective seven Federal troops defending the colors. When the fight was over, Tobe was the only one of the twelve living. For his gallantry, General Lee offered Tobe a first lieutenant's commission. However, Tobe refused because he had a speech impediment and was afraid that he could not issue commands adequately.

The Long's farm was in the northern part of the Palmetto community. After the Civil War, during the Reconstruction Era, William and Mary Catherine lived in the Edwards' home in Palmetto on the road from Verona. William was elected sheriff of what was then Pontotoc

County; Palmetto is now a part of Lee County that was later carved out of Itawambi and Pontotoc Counties. One story goes that Mary's husband had locked up a brutal murderer in the one room jail in the county seat. It was necessary for him to leave the community on business, and he left his wife in charge of the prisoner. The locals were not at all pleased with this particular murderer and decided in sheriff Long's absence to lynch him. It was late at night when a small, but angry, determined group of men approached the jail to break the prisoner out and hang him. They demanded that Mary hand over the keys. She met them on the front porch carrying a pistol and stood confronting them at the jailhouse door. After some argument and rowdiness, she announced that she would shoot any person trying to get at the prisoner. She raised the pistol, pointing it at the men, and one man was heard to say, "Watch out boys. She's redheaded and left handed." The crowd dispersed, and the prisoner lived to go to trial and was later hung.

There were six children born to Mary Catherine and William Long. Anna Hill was the oldest. My grandfather Charles Phillip was born four years after her on November 4, 1866. Samuel Edward, who later became an attorney in Atlanta, was born in 1868. Sam went on to practice law in Atlanta and died there during a plague epidemic. Sallie Lou only lived five years 1871- 1876. Mary Patty the last of the girls married into the A.H. Hutchinson family, and William Pearl, who later lived in Tupelo, was the youngest. My grandfather Long's family home was in the Palmetto, Mississippi community about three miles southwest of the town of Verona. The graveyard at the Palmetto Methodist Church still bares witness to all the Longs and Edwards who lived there before and after the Civil War. Many years later Uncle Pearl Long, my grandfather's youngest brother, wrote a short unpublished history of the Palmetto Church in which he said,

> The soil of Palmetto is sacred to me, for in the adjoining cemetery lie the earthly remains of both my grandfathers and grandmothers, my mother and father, two sisters and one brother, three maternal aunts, two paternal aunts, and two paternal uncles, and one uncle by marriage, J.N. McCord, one of the finest Christian gentlemen it has ever been my privilege to know. That fine Christian character, Mrs. Lucy McCord Yancy, a first cousin and childhood playmate, is resting a short distance from the front door or this church. Is it any wonder that this soil is sacred to me with all of these loved ones resting in it? These, besides friends of my boyhood days, naturally make it so.

Mary died July 17, 1910, and is buried there among the family and friends who made Palmetto an early center of life in Northeast Mississippi.

Palmetto and nearby Verona were the center of social and business life in that part of Northeast Mississippi. Palmetto was spread over the bottomland merger of red clay and black loam topsoils and white limestone outcroppings. Farming was good. It was home to a well-educated southern gentry, including some of the South Carolina Calhoun clan. The "old Calhoun place" which had been a hospital for wounded Confederate soldiers during the Civil War, was a tall, white, two-story mansion with English boxwood lining the long brick walkway from the iron-gate at the red clay road to the columned entrance of the grand house. It was pure Old South. When I was a child we would visit the cemetery, drive by the aged, unpainted one story remains of the Edward's home, and then drive down to the Calhoun place just to look at it. In my imagination as a child I could see the stretchers and the wounded lying around on the ground under the cedar trees and hear the moans and whispers of the dying. I even imagined the blood on the front porch and the black and white women with washbasins caring for the wounded. Whenever we went for a ride through the countryside on a Sunday afternoon, the old Calhoun place was never far from our minds. Later, when the Calhoun place was going to ruin like so many old ante bellum homes in Mississippi, my Aunt Olivia bought the hundred-year-old boxwood which lined the walk from the road to the house and had them dug up and replanted in our home in Tupelo. Eventually the remains of the old mansion burned. The shivery, culture, and pride of the old South was deeply engrained in Mama and our family. To understand Mary Bibb you have to understand her generation of southern women.

The bond between my grandfather and my mother was a bond of tenderness and love. Mother's bond with "The General," her mother, was a different sort of love and tenderness. It was a bond of steal, of will, of obedient loyalty, and above all, of dependent devotion. We never referred to Granny as the "The General" to her face. Among her peers and in the family she was known as Granny, Aunt Gus, Gussie, or Augusta Long. My mother addressed her early letters to her mother, "Dear Mither." Granny in turn signed her letters to my mother, "Mer," which caught on in their correspondence with one another. Her grand children, including myself, always referred to her as Granny. "The General" was no ordinary woman. The role she played in all of our lives was defining.

"The General" was born Augusta Lynn Holden in Lafayette, Georgia, March 9, 1869. Her father had married Augusta Bibb Campfield on Dec. 4, 1865; she was a child of a Civil War veteran and the Reconstruction Era. The Holden family was from middle Tennessee and seemed to have lost everything in the war. Shortly before her birth the family had moved in a wagon from Missionary Ridge in Chattanooga, Tennessee to Lafayette, Georgia. Their stay there was not long. They moved to Graysville, Georgia for a short time where her father's business failed. Augusta's father, Captain George Washington Holden, who had fought four years in the Civil War, died in Graysville when Augusta was ten. The family moved to Calhoun, Georgia. At her request Augusta went to Augusta, Georgia to begin the seventh grade when she was 14. In 1883 the family moved to Union County Mississippi to a home provided by an Uncle, Jim Thomas. Later the family moved permanently to Verona, Mississippi. I do not remember any conversations about my great-grandfather George Washington Holden, except that he served during the entire Civil War. He was in the cavalry of 45th Tennesse Regiment and fought in the Battle of Shiloh where he lost many of his friends. Once when I was in my teens, our immediate family was making a trip from Tupelo, Mississippi to Nashville, Tennessee, and my mother insisted that we leave the usual route and go out of our way in order to tour the Shiloh battlefield. She did not mention her grandfather's role in the battle, and all that

I can remember now of the event were the rolling hills, the changing leaves, the bronze plagues and military hardware that were on silent display. His unit was almost totally destroyed, and it was necessary to reorganize it with the 19th Tennessee Regiment that fought under General Forrest. Beyond those simple facts, and his marriage to Augusta Camfield, he remains a mystery to me. The Holden family, which I came to know, were all women; I never laid eyes on any of their husbands except my grandfather. Although there are pictures of the women from August Camfield on, I have not seen a picture of a single male in the Holden line.

Olivia Holden, born in 1859 was the oldest of the five girls; she married W.E Gray and returned in Chattanooga, which was his home. After they moved to Mississippi, Laura, who was older than Augusta, married a Mr. Leroy Taylor whose home was in Verona. His wife had died, and he already had two children by his first marriage. When Mr. Taylor's children were of age they left the Taylor home in Verona and played a very small role in our immediate family history. My memories of Aunt Laura's home included some of my favorite cousins, August Kincannon Trapp, Wibb, Augusta's husband, and Manna their daughter, who was a year or two older than my self. Wibb had a little fox terrier named Jap that he had taught every trick in the book. Jap was always good for a half hour of running, jumping, playing dead, rolling over, and playing catch. They lived with Aunt Laura, and "Gusta," as we called my cousin Augusta Trapp, took care of her. If Laura had any children by Mr. Taylor, they were not mentioned in any of the genealogical records of the family. Mr. Taylor himself is a shadow figure in the family lore as it was past to my generation. When we were children we often went down to "Aunt" Laura's home in Verona. She seemed to me to be very thin and very old at that time. When we stayed down at Aunt Laura's for any length of time, I would go by myself between the long row of big cedars, through the iron fence, and down the broken sidewalk several hundred yards to a small two-room house where my friend Jim Dawkins and his wife lived. Jim and his wife were black and had been with Aunt Laura for years and years. He was a handyman, and she was the family cook. I don't remember when we first became friends. I think it was when I was about four or five years old. All that I can remember now is going down to their small dark house that smelled of kerosene, and spending parts of afternoons with them. I was still very young and they reminded me of some of the people I had grown up with in China. As I grew older, they aged to the point that they no longer worked or took care of the house, but I enjoyed their hospitality and company.

Julia was the third daughter. I remember her as generous and loving to a fault. She literally gave away almost everything she had if she saw someone in need. If she had a flaw other than her generosity, it was dipping snuff. She used it profusely and enjoyed it immensely. There was no pretense about "Aunt Jule". Her coffee can that she spat in was neither far away nor out of sight. Aunt Jul married a Mr. J.B. Gibson, a farmer, who died before I got to know him. She took in a very young child, Laura Kellum, whose mother had died, and raised her like she was her own daughter. Laura loved her adopted family, and during her entire life, she and her family were an integral part of our entire family's life. After she married Dave Lawhon, she lived only a few miles away. She looked after Aunt Jul as if she were her mother. Tom Gibson, Aunt Jul's only child by Mr. Gibson, moved a considerable distance away from Tupelo when he was an adult. He and his wife Leola spent a month's vacation at my grandmother's in Tupelo every summer, the only time we saw or heard from them. Aunt Jul lived in the Brewer Community about five miles southeast of Verona in a small side by side duplex that my grandfather built for her after a tornado ripped away her modest home. She lived on several acres of land. Just in the bend of the road before you got to her place there were several huge blackberry and plumb thickets. Back behind the house was a large grove of scallybark hickory trees. Each spring early on a Saturday morning we would go down to the Brewer Community, and pick wild blackberries and plums so that my mother and "The General" could make jams and jellies. The chiggers were awesome. If you have never had chigger bites up and down your legs, in your crotch, and on your body, you will never imagine what hell is like. We were miserable for days, even after we had applied lard and salt to the bites. In the fall we would go down the wagon road back of the house and pick up scaly-bark nuts for Christmas fruitcakes. The air down among the trees had a fall, dusty, leafy, hickory smell. There was always an older couple living on the other side of the house; they cultivated the acreage, cut the firewood, and generally took care of things. Aunt Jul had a rocker that she sat in out on the front porch of the house. I still have her rocking chair that had been rocked so long that the rockers were flat on the bottoms. I recaned it a number of years ago. All that one can possibly do with it is to move one's body back and forth because the chair won't rock.

Augusta Lynn was the third daughter. "The General" was the family leader, although I think that Laura her older sister was more of a presence during their younger years. Laura was exceptionally well read. She learned French on her own and was the more intellectual of the daughters. Julia married Mr. Gibson before she could get an education beyond Verona public schools, and they moved to Brewer to farm. Augusta, at the ripe age of eighteen entered the first all women's college in the United States, Mississippi Industrial College for Women later known as Mississippi State College for Women. M.S.C.W. was located in Columbus, Mississippi about fifty miles way. When she graduated, "Granny" as we called her to her face took a contract to teach schools in the Piney Woods of south Mississippi where, for all practical purposes, she was shut off from family and the entire outside world. She was the school. There were no real roads in and out of the Piney Woods. You went in on a horse or a wagon that might or might not follow the ruts of a previous wagon. Once you were there, you were on your own. You lived with a family to which you were assigned and shared their poverty, joys, and failures. The community was extremely poor. But they knew how to celebrate. Granny used to tell about a three-day wedding where everyone for miles around came and fiddled, danced, ate, and celebrated the marriage. There was little cleared farmland in the Piney Woods, and serious logging had not yet begun. Most people lived off a small plot that they tilled and from hunting and fishing. In spite of the poverty, they were a proud people and attempted to bring the very best education that they could to the woods. There was infrequent mail that was periodically collected and carried out to the nearest town where in coming mail was collected and send on by the next person going into the Piney Woods.

The General lived to be ninety-nine years old; she died six weeks before her one hundredth birthday. Her influence on everyone mentioned in this collection of stories was profound. It was not until we came home from China on furlough that she began to have a direct impact on my own life. Part of that impact was the stories of the Piney Woods, which will be chronicled later on.

Annie Holden was the youngest, and some say the prettiest of the family. She married a Mr. Kincannon whose first wife had died and left him with three children. Annie provided him with more. They lived in Oxford, the cultural center of North Mississippi and the home of the University of Mississippi. Of all my cousins the Kincannons were by far the most colorful, and fun loving. They knew everyone in Oxford including the Faulkners. Oliver Kincannon and William Faulkner grew up together as good friends. Oliver is best known in the family lore, not for his friendship with William Faulkner, but for a once in a lifetime performance at the traditional Thanksgiving football game between Old Miss and Mississippi State. Oliver and a number of his friends were thoroughly enjoying the game and the basic bleacher game of passing the bottle. It seems that after Oliver had consumed not a little spirits, he decided to enter the football game. He jumped from the bleachers, ran onto the field, picked up the ball, and zigzagged his way through both teams trying to catch him into one end zone and then, for good measure, proceeded to reverse direction and score at the other end of the field. Having scored his points he climbed one of the goal posts refusing to come down until the local police hauled him off to jail for the night to sober up.

Life in Verona was not at all bad. The town had a rich social life. Much of the town's social life took place around the Baptist and Methodist churches. I only remember seeing the Holden home place in Verona on one occasion in the early 1940s, and it was already is considerable disrepair. Its last occupants were tenant farmers who worked a small acreage on the edge of town.

After several years of living in the very primitive conditions of the back woods of southern Mississippi, Augusta returned to Verona and the following year married my grandfather. One of my mother's cousins, the daughter of Pearl Long my grandfathers younger brother, told me shortly before she died in 1999, that Augusta came back from the Piney Woods hoping to marry Sam Long, my grandfathers older brother; but things unexplained happened, and she married Charles Phillip Long of Palmetto. Augusta married well.

My grandfather was born in 1866 the last year of the Civil War and grew up during the Reconstruction Era. The period was difficult to say the least. The weight of defeat and grief over losses of family, friends, and possessions after the Civil War was not nearly as bad as the simple business of making a daily living. Almost everyone was poor, both black and white. No one really knew what to do. Farming started back slowly. Because most, but certainly not all, of the freed blacks were illiterate, many of them wound up back on the farms at low wages or as sharecroppers. In the early years many whites did as poorly as the blacks.

There simply were no jobs and the farms that had been left untended during the war were in awful shape. Livestock was short, and because horse and mules were conscripted during the war, they were far from plentiful. It would take years before the land became profitable again. Whites and blacks were exploited by "carpetbaggers," opportunists who had come to the South to seek their fortunes, or by "scallywags," southern opportunists who took advantage of whomever they could. The surface of society was civil, but violence was just under the surface. On the local level it was difficult to maintain law and order. Vigilantly groups dealt out justice as they interpreted it.

Uncle Pearl use to tell a story about a band of horse thieves that worked all the way from Georgia to Texas. They would steal the horses in one state and drive them across several states and sell them. According to Uncle Pearl, it was not uncommon for them to steal the same horses several times. Warned that the band was passing through the Palmetto area, people began guarding their barns. Two boys John Calhoun and Jim McFarland were guarding the Calhoun barn when two men came into the barn and bridled several horses and mules. As they headed out of the barnyard the boys challenged them and the thieves opened fire. The boys returned fire with their shotguns loaded with slugs and killed one of the intruders and wounded the second. On the morning after a posse was made up to trail the wounded thief. The posse was headed by highly thought of Confederate Veterans, Capt. William Cunningham, Lt. Philip Long, and Addison Davis, all physically big and bewhiskered men. They found the man near the Palmetto school. The dying man confessed to his role in the thieving ring and told the posse that the rest of the group planned a rendezvous west of Birmingham Ridge. The posse moved secretly through the night and surrounded the spot just before daybreak. Seventeen men we caught. A jury was selected, a trial held, and a verdict of guilty pronounced. However, at this point Capt. Jim Dillard, the highly respected Lee County Sheriff, arrived and took charge of the prisoners. Since there was no jail to hold the prisoners, Dillard set out with them for the Monroe County jail. In conference the posse decided that they did not what the prisoners to leave their County jurisdiction, so they intercepted the group a few miles south of Tupelo and hanged all seventeen of them from a single large oak tree.

Another story that I was told when I was teaching at the University of Central Arkansas was about a distant cousin of ours who had been swindled by a "carpetbagger," and in the argument that followed killed the man. He was arrested and tried. The cousin was found guilty of murder and sentenced to be hung. Mysteriously he died the night before the execution and his body was carried out the jail in a coffin and buried. In 1968 I discovered that he had in fact "escaped" to Arkansas and that his grandson was the editor of one of the local paper.

Growing up during the Reconstruction Era was difficult. The political issues were so complex that the formation of a local government was slow and often painful. Blacks gained their freedom during the war and the right to vote after the war. But the formation of an equitable and just society was far from complete. Within fifteen years Blacks had for all practical purposes lost their right to vote because states enacted poll tax and literacy tests to vote. The animosity of both races went underground to erupt off and on in what became a segregated society. Poor Whites were not much better off than Blacks. Many of them were also illiterate and poorly trained. "The White trash," as they were called, wound up as sharecroppers or day laborers with very meager incomes and absolutely no social status. For many of the poor whites and their children education was a luxury they could not afford. Everyone had to work, or the family starved. What saved the average Southerner were the expansion of the railroad and the rise of the industrial South. Those who couldn't wait for the transformation headed west.

My grandfather Charles was tall, about six feet three or four inches. He was thin, had a fairly large nose, a big head of hair, searching eyes, and an eloquent voice. He seems to have been less than a fancy dresser; in fact he looked dowdy most of the time, his cloths hanging on him like a scarecrow. In his wedding pictures, however, he looked both hansom and well dressed. He had gone to school in Palmetto and later in Verona under a high respected teacher, A. A. Kincannon. To continue his education Charles began his college life at the Agricultural and Mechanical College in Starkville (Mississippi State University), but he got homesick, and came back to Palmetto. After a year he transferred to Old Miss, the University of Mississippi, where he finished his degree in law. In 1885 he moved to Tupelo, but did not begin his law practice until 1888. When he arrived in Tupelo, Charles was taken in as a legal clerk by an older attorney, General James L. Finley, who was then the District Attorney. He not only clerked for Finley but lived in but lived in Finley's home. Later my grandfather formed the firm of Long and Anderson with another promising young lawyer, W. D.

Anderson. Years later The Tupelo Journal stated that for many years no case went to trial in Lee County without the Long-Anderson firm serving as either the defense or the prosecution. Anderson would eventually serve on the Mississippi Supreme Court. In 1918 my grandfather ran for Circuit Court Judge of the First Judicial District of Mississippi, an office that he held until 1930. It was said of him that he set a record in the cost of dispatching the business of the court and in the minimum number of cases reversed or remanded by the State Supreme Court.

Prior to the 1930's election he presided over a trial of a black man who was a tenant farmer on a farm belonging to a prominent north Mississippi family. The farm raised watermelons, and during the preceding year the harvest had been badly hit by thieves. The owner of the farm had instructed his tenant farmer to shoot anyone who came into the field to take the melons. As it happened the owner himself came one night to get a watermelon, and in the dark the tenant shot him and he died. There was considerable clamor with racial overtones for vengeance. The tenant was tried by a jury and found guilty of murder. Under the state guidelines the presiding Judge had the discreassion of sentencing the man to death or to send him to the State Prison. My grandfather refused to give the man the death penalty and sent him to the Penitentiary. His refusal to give the death sentence became the central issue of the 1930s election. My grandfather lost. He returned to his law practice in Tupelo and was joined by his oldest son Sam. He continued to practice law in Tupelo till his death in 1938. From the time he served as Circuit judge until his death he continued to be known as Judge Long. As much as thirty years after his death, I was often introduced to people around Tupelo as Judge Long's grandson.

Tupelo originally belonged to the Chickasaw Indians. Some of the land that now is the center of the business district was bought from Pis-tah-lah-tubby, a Chickasaw chief. There was no town at the current sight until around 1859; there was only a cluster of communities that extended from the Natchez Trace on the east and north to the Tombigbee River on the east. Much of the area which was to make up the business district was marshland and not suitable for a town until it was drained. Gradually a few stores, taverns and hotels appeared along the railroad tracks and the community took on the name Gum Pond for the small lake and gum trees north of where the town was forming.

As the town took shape churches were built and the population grew to about 100 people in 1864. In 1867 it was chosen to be the new county seat for Lee County because of its central location. By 1880 Tupelo had grown to about 1000 people. Tupelo had its first member of the U.S Congress, "Private" John Allen, who was elected in 1884 and was reelected for 16 years. At the end of the century Tupelo's population topped 1500. By that time my grandfather had become one of the town leading citizens and entrepreneurs. Not only was he a successful lawyer, but he was instrumental along with a number of other young community leaders to help found the Tupelo Cotton Mill which eventually produced as much as twenty miles of cloth a day. In 1902 he and another group of men raised money to build a modern fertilizer factory to enhance the new agriculture practices developing across the South.

He became the President of the Cotton Belt And Tupelo Fertilizer Factory. He and his friends were responsible for a Civil War memorial that stood at the intersection of Main and Monument Streets and was later moved the courthouse lawn. With a number of other city leaders the "Judge" helped to raise money for a Y.M.C.A. building that was built on Main Street. It later became Tupelo's first hospital. In his law practice he represented a number of Tupelo enterprises including the McGuire Spoke Factory that turned out 3,000,000 spokes a year. The spokes factory delivered spokes as far away as Germany. On one occasion my grandfather was supposed to go to Dusseldorf, Germany to represent the Mcguire's interest. He got as far as New York and turned back. The train ride had made him ill and the idea of crossing the Atlantic was too much. He returned to Tupelo and settled the matter by mail.

By the time my grandparents married in 1893 Tupelo had become the center of life for North East Mississippi. Verona had lost out to Tupelo in 1887 in an aggressive campaign to get the Memphis, Birmingham & Atlanta (Frisco) railroad to cross the Gulf Mobil and Ohio (GM&O) in their town. Palmetto and the other small communities around the area had not developed extensive business areas. In 1885 Tupelo had been nothing but a small stretch of buildings along the GM&O railroad. Two years later it was selected by the Lee County voters to be the County seat because of its central location. Tupelo had welcomed both the Gulf Mobil and Ohio and the Frisco railroads, and they crossed on the southeastern edge of town. The GM&O went north and south connecting the Ohio Valley with the Gulf of Mexico; and the Frisco went east and west connecting Memphis, Tennessee and the western frontier with Birmingham, Alabama and Atlanta.

Both of my grandparents' families had been pillars of Palmetto Methodist Church. The Rev. William Augustus Campfield, one of my great-great-grandfathers on my grandmother's side, had pastored the church at one time. But by the time my grandparents married on April 12th, 1893 at the Baptist Church in Verona, Augusta's family was all Baptists. Charles had never been very religious. In his typical way of making light of things, his excuse had been that when he was growing up the family only had meat on Sunday and that was chicken. On Sundays the minister was always invited to eat lunch and there was never enough chicken for all the children. Being thus deprived, he was not inclined to be active in the Church. Although in its early years Tupelo had several churches, they were served by itinerate preachers who usually came once a month. People went to one another's churches on the other Sundays. Revivals were community events at which prominent evangelist preached for a week or so. According to my Grandmother, it was at "The Cate's meeting that my Grandfather joined the Baptist Church "after confessing his Savior." He was immersed by Bro. Kimbrough on August 10th or the 11th. The "General" had been a children's leader in the First Baptist Church for years. Eventually, both of my grandparents became active members in the First Baptist Church. "The General" prevailed.

There was never a question as to who ran the home in Tupelo. Charles practiced law and was an entrepreneur. He provided well for his family and in the family lore was the fun loving, light side of family life, although in all of the pictures of him that I have seen, he is never smiling. I think of him as a melancholy jokester with an extra ordinary dry wit and a consummate command of words. Augusta commanded the house single mindedly, and provided the stability for the family. Granny was not austere, but wherever she happened to be she was a presence. Whether it was at church, at a social gathering, or at home, everyone was aware of her when she entered the room.

The General's life from the time of their marriage till the last child went off to school was having babies and taking care of her family and church. Sam, who was my grandmother's favorite, was born in 1894, the year after my grandparent's marriage, mother in December of 1895, Julia in 1897, Charles Jr. in 1900, and Olivia in 1904. In 1898 Charles and Augusta bought a lot in Tupelo on Jefferson Street from a Mr. Rice. The address 543 Jefferson was to become a symbol of family solidarity and tradition. Things were not easy for the couple during their early years of marriage. My grandfather was continuously busy, and a good part of his life depended upon his socializing with other men in town. Tupelo was known not only for its churches but also its saloons. There was a period in the family's life when my grandfather had to deal with too much alcohol. According to two separate stories which have been past down, his problems with alcohol ended abruptly. My Aunt Olivia said that it ended with his making a huge mistake with a case he was handling. According to my Aunt he is purported to have said that he might as well have been, "buck naked running wild in the bottom land with a feather in his tail." The other story, which I heard from my grandmother, was that he came home inebriated the day my Aunt Olivia was born in 1904. It was a time that you gave birth to your babies at home. Granny had been in labor all day long, and her physician, Dr. Bonner, had stayed the whole time at the house. The day after Olivia's birth my grandfather did not remember any of the events that had occurred. From that time on swore he would never drink again. Whatever the real reason, he abruptly stopped drinking and did not pick the habit up again. In fact after prohibition became the law of the land, he was known as a judge who would enforce the law fully.

In the later 1890s Tupelo was a town with dirt streets kept somewhat level by road graders that were pulled by several teams of horses. Every one kept a horse, mules or a pony to ride or pull their carriages and wagons. Everyone seems to have had a cow. The back part of 543 Jefferson had an unpretentious barn and grazing plot. In each yard there was either a windmill and a trough or a pump that was operated manually. Some people had both. Water was carried in buckets or basins into the house for use. Needless to say there was not any indoor plumbing. In door plumbing was soon to come in the early 1900s, as was electricity. The city water works, sewerage system, and power plant were some of the first of their kind in the region. Electricity was severely limited, but it was there. It was this early development of electrical power in Tupelo that later gave it an advantage over other towns when it was chosen by the Tennessee Valley Authority to be the first TVA town. The first automobiles were introduced in Tupelo in 1906. By this time Tupelo, for economic reasons, had extended its roads to several miles outside the city limits; it was just good for business. Congressman John

Allen ran as "Private Allen" because so many others were running as General, Captain, etc. His home was just across Madison Street from the property that my grandparents bought and lived. "Private" John Allen was responsible for bring the first national fish hatchery to Tupelo. In his speech before congress he declared there were millions of little fish dying to be born in Tupelo. This was all happening as my mother was growing up as a child.

The first house at 543 Jefferson burned down. Fire was a major problem in Tupelo. All that was available at the time was a bucket brigade, and it seldom succeeded in putting out a fire unless the blaze was caught early. My Aunt Olivia says that it was my grandmother's level-headedness and command of the situation when the first house burned that was the beginning of her title, the "General." A second house was built on the 543 Jefferson lot. It was a two story Victorian house with porches on three sides set in the middle of what would become a circle of large oak trees. It would be home for the whole family until the Tupelo Tornado in 1936.

Sam was the first born, and his mother favorite. He was a fun loving mischievous boy, who did well enough at school, but was more interested in football, basketball and sports than he was in academics. My Grandmother duly recorded that he "confessed Christ as his Savior" and joined the Baptist Church during a revival in September of 1906. Although in his retirement years he was very outspoken in the Baptist Church, even to the point of standing up during a sermon and correcting the minister, during most of his adult life, church was quite secondary.

When my Uncle Sam Long went to Old Miss, he was not far from family; Sam had a particularly strong friendship with his cousin Oliver Kincannon and got to know Oliver's friends, which included William Faulkner. Sam's daughter told me that on one occasion after his graduation from Old Miss, her father, who had just married, took his wife Genevieve up to the Faulkner's home uninvited. Like any good southern hostess, Mrs. Faulkner invited them in. Sam and his wife stayed a rather long time, so that, as super time came around, they were graciously invited to eat. However, as they were about to leave the living room there was a terrible racket upstairs that went on and on. Finally Mrs. Faulkner explained that William had been on a three-day bender, that there was a telephone call for him, and they were trying to get him to come to the phone. The afternoon uninvited visit was over.

World War I changed the lives of everyone in the Long family. Sam had finished Old Miss with a degree in law and came home to practice with his father. However, the U.S. entered World War I about this time, and Sam enlisted in the Army on May the eight, 1917. He did his basic training near Forth Smith Arkansas at the Officers Training Camp at Ft Logan H. Roots. Upon finishing his officer's training he was commissioned a 2nd Lieutenant. This was followed by two weeks at home before he reported to Camp Pike in Little Rock where he trained enlisted men. In December he was promoted to 1st Lieutenant.

My grandmother wrote in her notebook,

> Charlie and I went over to Camp Pike Feb. 13th, found Sam in hospital. . . . Sam spent ten days

at home the later part of March –convalescing. We had a most delightful time. Found expression for our pent-up feelings in some rare old poems-which Sam read aloud to his "Mer." Long will they linger as sweet memories. The visit of May 30, 31, and June 1st was not satisfactory. We could not overcome the dread of the long farewell we must so soon take. Many minuets even hours passed uneasily – little said. We were unnatural. Sam left at 5 o'clock June 2nd/ 18. Returning to Camp Pike.

Josephine Lillie and I went over to Camp Pike – Sat. eve. June 8th. Monday night – I kissed my boy good bye – standing in the middle of the aisle of the sleeper.

Sam left for Camp Dix June sixteenth. His first letter came June twenty sixth – On the fifteenth of July Sam and Genevieve were married. Letters from them arrived Aug. tenth. A telegram saying Sam would sail on Sun. the twenty fifth came Sat. the twenty fourth. My grandmother wrote,

> And now that time has come and Sam has very likely stepped upon the ship that will bear him away – and this will be his first night to be rocked in the cradle of the Deep – I have committed his keeping to his maker and his God. Asking Him to continue his loving kindness and enable me to accept whatever comes –as the kindest – most loving and wise disposal –a loving father could grant."

While he was in Arkansas Sam had met Genevieve Mathis in Little Rock. Genevieve's family was Canadian. I have never known exactly why they were living in Little Rock. Genevieve was just seventeen when they married and Sam was shipped over seas. In World War I he served in Company D of the 347 Regiment of the 801 Division of the U.S. Infantry. Although Sam came back to Tupelo in 1918 and went into law practice with his father, his real joy and interest in life was in the military. In W.W. II he rose to the rank of Lt. Col. and commanded an artillery battalion in North Africa, Italy and Germany. The trip across the Atlantic was quite eventful. He was on two ships which were hit by torpedoes and on one of these occasions, I am told, drew his pistol to keep the men under his command from jumping overboard before they were rescued. He was considered extremely lucky by his men because they never suffered a single casualty from enemy fire. He did lose one battery when a faulty shell exploded in the breech of one of the guns. I am told that when the company began to fire again after the accident, that he stood behind the first gun that was fired because the men were afraid of the faulty ordinance. At the end of the war he was a full Col. and remained in Germany in an advisory capacity to the formation of the new German government. He remained in the National Guard after he left active duty and eventually rose to the rank of Brig. General and was second in command of the Mississippi National Guard.

The matriarchal nature of our clan shaped my mother, Bibb. She was born the next to the last day of 1895, December thirtieth. From early childhood she was destined to excel. She was by all accounts, her mother's, sisters', and other relatives, the "perfect" daughter. Mary Bibb made a profession of faith and was baptized when she was ten years old. The following year she made it be known that she was going to be a missionary. In later years mother would claim that her decision had been made while she was in the Sunbeams at the First Baptist Church. Granny was in charge of the Sunbeams, the Women's Missionary Union organization for small children. Among the odds and ends I found in an old box was a post card size award with four little Easter chickens pictured on it, given to Mary Bibb for perfect attendance at Sunbeams by August Long, her mother. It was not remarkable for a small child in Sunbeams to be moved by stories of missionaries and announce that they were going to far away lands to serve God as a missionary. Mother grew up on stories of missionary heroes and martyrs. However, with mother her declaration was more than a passing childhood fantasy. Her affirmation marked the beginning of a determined goal in life.

Mother never gave her parents a single cause to be concerned about her character or her intelligence. From the first years of her schooling till she finished Tupelo High School she was an exemplary student. She was the Secretary and Treasurer for the High School debating society which among other things debated whether women should be given the vote in Mississippi, and I do not know how many times my younger sister and I were reminded when we were in High School that mother had been valedictorian of her class. It was not until we were in college that we discovered that there were only six students in her entire class. My younger sister reminded me that, although there were only six people in her class, her close friend Oline Coffee, who later became the principal of Tupelo Elementary School was academically right on her heels.

Mary Bibb was bright and like many educated young women of her day she became interested in the classics. When she finished Tupelo High School she enrolled at Mississippi Industrial College for Women, better known as Mississippi State College for Women. Her mother had attended there when she was a young woman. Bibb was there for a year and transferred to the University of Mississippi as an English and Classics major. At that time it was quite out of the ordinary for women to enroll in the University of Mississippi, there were fewer than five women in her class at Old Miss. She chose to go to the University of Mississippi rather a women's college because she saw herself as a serious scholar who could do as well as a man on any academic level. Mother was never such a strong feminist that she saw herself in competition with men. However, some of her closest friends were active in the women's suffrage movement, and some of them chose to be single because it was thought at the time that one could not really have a career and be a married women as well. Mother just wanted the challenge of the University and wanted to get the best teaching available. Her love of the classics was to be my burden in High School. She insisted that I take Latin, the only course that I ever failed. While I was failing Latin, she was reveling in a course in Biblical Greek that was being taught in Chinese at the Chinese Baptist Seminary on our compound in Shanghai.

Julia was born two years after mother and was barely one year old when the first house burned. There is not much in the family lore about Julia's childhood. I know she had the same exposure to Sunbeams and the church that my mother had, but it did not have the same effect. Julia always enjoyed life. Although she had a serious side about her, the part you always noticed was the fun loving side. She enjoyed dating and seeing boys and doesn't seem to have been particularly anxious about academics, though she did well enough. When Julia finished Tupelo High School she decided to get further way from home than Old Miss or MSCW. She packed up her things and entered Shorter College in Georgia. The war was on and she met a young Lieutenant, Dan Dean while she was visiting in New Orleans and the two proceeded to elope. Dan's family, who were Spanish in background, were good Roman Catholics, but this did not seem to bother Julia. When Dan left the military, he and Julia moved to Bayonne, New Jersey where Dan was a reporter of the Bayonne Times. Julia began working in the women's department at Franklin Simon's Department store in New York. They lived in a predominately Jewish community. Both of them loved it and made life long friendships with a number of their neighbors. Later in life. when Julia and Dan had moved to Tupelo and 543 Jefferson, she would make an annual trip to New York to see her friends and buy women's wear for the store in Tupelo where she worked. Often their New York friends would come south to visit them.

Mother's second brother, Charles Phillip Long Jr. was born in 1900 when she was five. The General now had four children under 10 years old. Uncle Charles was named well. He looked like his father, tall (about six three or four), slender, full head of hair and an easy smile. He and Julia were a lot alike in personality and were always close to one another. Charles was quite an athlete in Tupelo High School and later played football at Old Miss. He entered Old Miss when he was nineteen, and was a sophomore when Mary Bibb went to China. After finishing a law degree at Old Miss, he practiced law in Pontotoc, about twenty miles west of Tupelo, for a few years. Charles Jr. did not really enjoy practicing law and became a claims adjustor for an insurance company. The company sent him down to the Mississippi coast where he met my Aunt Enid, who was undoubtedly the most gracious person I have ever known. Enid Roland was the daughter of the British consul in New Orleans, an Episcopalian, and very proud of her Welch heritage. They were married in 1928 and moved to Tupelo. Sam had bought a dairy farm and Charles went into business with his brother. It was not a congenial arrangement.

Tom, Charles' and Enid's first son, was born in Tupelo in 1929. At one point Charles thought that he might go into the chicken farming business, but this venture did not turn out well. He, Enid, and Tom moved back to the Gulf Coast, and Uncle Charles went back into the insurance business in 1931.

Olivia was the youngest of the children and the most whimsical and creative. She too underwent Sunbeams and the General's religious training, but she seems to have always been an independent spirit. Olivia use to tell that her mother once characterized her children in a small diary like book that she discovered. "Sam", the General said, "was a loveable baby, a fine boy, brave soldier, good scholar. . .; Mary Bibb was a precious child, so obedient, so attentive, so scholarly. . .; Julia was not too pretty at birth, but grew into a beautiful child, so sweet, so obedient, so loveable. . .; Charles was a little slow at first, but developed rapidly, sweet and adorable, very frank. . .; Olivia had a cat named Daizelle that lived to be fourteen years old." Olivia did not need to be spoiled as the youngest child; she simply did her own thing, which was usually imaginative and different. When she finished school in Tupelo, she went to Baylor Female College (Mary Harding Baylor College) in Temple Texas for three years where she was in constant trouble for breaking the rules. At Mary Harding Baylor she changed the spelling of her name to Olyvya. She transferred to Baylor University in Waco where she received her undergraduate degree in speech as Olyvya Long. Olyvya had a variety of interests. In one of her few letters to her mother she mentioned that she had a part on one of the school plays, "The Little Stone House," and she also was playing competitive basketball and volleyball. She tutored some high school students in "declamation." One of her high school students got a second place award in her school. "Liv" loved to play bridge and dated quite a bit. She had plans to work in summer camp, but it was not clear as to whether or not she ever did. By this time she had already developed a life long love for plants and flowers, and sent four varieties of cactus to her mother with instruction on how to plant them, and with whom to share them. On a trip to Eastland, Texas "Liv" saw some beautiful purple Chinese lilac bushes and vowed to buy some roots from the people who owned them. Almost two pages of her three-page letter were taken up with flowers and how the late rains and frost had killed the vegetation and ruined the fruit crop. She ended the letter asking whether Aunt Julia had planted the dogwoods and redbuds that she had

was six feet four or five inches tall. She reported that she weighted 133 pounds and was getting up early to read her Bible, take a sponge bath, drink a tumbler of water and take "physical cultures" before breakfast. Her pressing desire was to be in Tupelo and take part in the W.M.U.; she had not been to a single meeting in Summit because it conflicted with her schoolwork. She missed being in the Church in Oxford where she was made to feel at home, but thought that one of the reasons was that she had not yet moved her church membership to Summit. Already she was looking forward to Christmas and being at home. She was having serious doubts about teaching another year in Summit, and suggested that she would go on to the W.M.U. Training School.

Mother's social life in Summit wasn't bad at all. She told her mother that she had been invited by a Mr. Newman after Sunday School to go down to the river with the Covington girls and himself. They took with them a wonderful picnic dinner of fried chicken, sandwiches, fruits, cake, and raisin bread. After eating they waded a while and then drove around until five in the afternoon. She had just gotten bathed and cleaned up to go to church when one of the Covington's phoned and asked her if she would like to go riding again, this time in a Buick with two of Summit's young male socialites. They missed church and stayed out until eleven. One of her co-workers teased her all week about her piety and called her a back-slider for missing church. It seems that Mr. Newman turned out to be a good friend. Coming home from the Post Office with him one day, Mother thought that she had pulled a very good joke on him when she asked him if his possum had died. When he asked why, she replied, "I see you are doing your own grinning." It became a standing joke between them. Going for a ride and picnicking after church on Sunday was one of the primary forms of social gatherings in Summit, and Bibb went often with various families and young friends.

Mary Bibb was not above pulling practical jokes. She wrote, "Every-one is excited over the election here- we had ten vote the Republican ticket and about a hundred and forty the Democratic. I've been making out I'm a Republican to cause a stir." Sometimes the tables were turned on her. She thought that a visiting Presbyterian Elder was complimenting her when he said that she looked like Helen Kellar, especially her eyes and mouth. But then he continued by saying, "When we saw her (Helen Kellar) I had to carry my little son home, she gave Dr. Cooper and me the jim-jaws and my fifteen year old daughter would not sleep alone for 8 months." Mother was appalled

Her students were anything but a joke for her. In one of her November letters she complained that the children had been on a tare all week, and that she had ". . .resolved to whip a few if they worry me again tomorrow. Mr. Bedwell (her fellow married teacher) says it will cure them somewhat." When the first and second grade children asked her to play "Bear" with them, she obliged and tripped over a root in the school yard, skinning her knee and hurt her finger, ". . . but didn't tear my hose." After that she resorted to telling stories to the children during recess which turned out to be a very popular event. At the end of the semester she was no less home sick; but she seems to have gotten along much better, especially with the older students. She did have to abide a few "dunces" who gave her a hard time.

By the end of the year she was quite uncertain as to whether or not she would return to Summit. I found a highly complimentary recommendation by a Summit attorney, Will Parsons, written in May of 1917 that indicated that she might be looking for another position. However, mother did return to Summit for another two years.

She had made friends with a several of young women both at the University of Mississippi and at Blue Mountain College, a Baptist women's college in Blue Mountain, Mississippi. Her friendships at Blue Mountain with both students and faculty were to last a lifetime. Although she never attended Blue Mountain, I think she thought of herself as a Blue Mountain graduate. The decision to go the Baptist W.M.U. Training School was simply a natural step in the direction she was already going. Mother had wanted to get a Masters degree, and my grandfather promised her that he would send her to Columbia University or any other University of her choosing, if she really wanted to go.

In her "Sketch of Mary Bibb. . ." my grandmother wrote:

> In the mean time, Mary Bibb was corresponding with the Foreign Mission Board Office from which body she learned that two years of training at the University in Louisville, (actually the W.M.U. Training School) was required of aspirants to the foreign fields.

> Her father's reaction to this gave Mary Bibb one of, if not, the hardest decisions to make, when he stated he would give the Columbia course or that at Louisville, perhaps not realizing its weight. She went up stairs to fight it out. Coming down later, the Training School had been chosen, giving up her aspirations for a masters degree, seemingly of personal gratification, though, we all know a servant of God can not have too great store of knowledge (sic).

About the time that Olivia finished High School, Sam had come home from the war. He and Genevieve had their first child in 1919, whom they named Genevieve. Julia and Dan were in Bayonne, New Jersey. Charles was enrolled at Old Miss. Mother entered the W.M.U. Training School and was preparing to go to the mission field.

At one point my grandfather told her he would give $10,000.00 dollars too foreign missions if she would not go. For that day and time it was a large sum of money and really not one that he could afford. My grandmother wrote that she thought to herself that that much money might be more helpful to foreign missions than any contribution my mother might make on the mission field. However, mother's answer sent a thrill down her spine. According to my grandmother, my mother tearfully told her father. "But, Papa, that would be your work, I must do mine." Needless to say he was quite moved.

My Grandfather had an ally in the pastor of the First Baptist Church who called on my mother shortly after her decision in order to dissuade her. After dwelling on my Grandfather's health, which was not very good at the time, he advised her to stay at home and take care of him. Her pastor told her that he "did not place much stress on calls." He said, "If he had been definitely called, he did not know it." Then he added, "You may have just worked yourself up to believing you have been called by God, being missled (sic) by the excitement of going to China." My Grandmother stated: "With amazement in her eyes and voice she replied, "She knew God had called. He (God) knowing then, the things would come to pass when time came to go, and unless The Lord changed the call, releasing her in a clear way, she had no choice, but to accept.(sic)" According to my grandmother, mother then went on to recall Jesus' reply to the man who was not ready to obey- "The dead must bury the dead, but you follow me.(sic)."

What Bibb's pastor did not know was that she had written in a letter to her father about his health and personal problems after she had been home from the W.M.U. Training School at Christmas time in 1920.

> You do know know (sic) how much it hurts me to see you sick, nervous and discouraged, it casts a depressing spell over my spirits and I hardly feel like smiling or being happy. I could as far as I'm concerned individually throw off the spell, but my heart aches to think that you are suffering- and yet I think much of your distress could be relieved if you trusted Christ with your affairs rather than try to bear all your burdens yourself. Papa, I know you are a Christian, but if one can judge by actions I think you have lost the joy of your salvation. I do not mean to be impudent or take advantage of

you because I'm writing and you can't reply, but I've thought and prayed over the matter and my conclusion is that there is some barrier between you and the Father and you cannot see His face, feel his presence and know that you are working in partnership with Him who has loved, redeemed you and given you His message of love and grace to give unto others. There are several things that make me feel this. The fact that you can sit and play solitaire which(sic) worship is going on, even on Sunday, you do not take an interest in the salvation of others, at least to the degree that you go after them as you used to do, you give but you do not do it with cheerfulness, in other words, you are not living the Christ like life. It may be that you have never forgiven Mr. Ledyard and those connected with the cotton mill affair. Is that true? I think maybe after the affair your faith in men in general was tried severely and perhaps suffered. If you have not forgiven those who did misunderstand and mistrust you, you can't expect God to forgive you.' If ye forgive not men their trespasses, neither will your heavenly father forgive you your trespasses.

In the letter she went on to chide him,

'But seek ye first the Kingdom of God and His righteousness and all these things (food, drink, clothing) shall be added to you.' 'Again, commit thy way unto the Lord, trust also in Him, and he shall bring it to pass.' '<u>Trust</u> in the Lord, and do good; so shalt thou dwell in the land, and verily thou shalt be fed. Delight in the Lord; and He shall give thee the desires of thine heart.' By our failure to trust we question the truth of our Lord and dishonor Him, and when we worry and are over anxious about money and worldly or earthly matters we are making the Master's burden heavier as well as dishonoring Him by lack of faith. Won't you surrender yourself and reconscrate your life to Him?

. . . . I hope you will see that I don't mean to be upish or say anything a child should not to her parent, but that <u>I love you</u> and want you to have the same peace of heart and mind and joy in life and service, I have. Forgive me, if I offend.

Although the letter was written with genuine devotion by a loving daughter, how deeply it added to my Grandfather's depression, one can only guess. He seemed to have understood and loved his daughter too much for this letter to create a breach between them. The letter, however, was an indication of how my mother would face all of her own problems during the rest of her life.

At the end of February she wrote her mother at the Gartly-Ramsey Hospital in Memphis. It is not clear who was hospitalized. The letter was a heart felt love letter to both parents in which she included two poems. The first, which I think she composed herself, was addressed to both of them.

If I could write what I thought,
Or could say just what I ought,

81

> I'd write a world that's all pure gold.
> That never on the lips is cold.
> There's not a world, no not another
> That means as much as just this –
> Mother
> I love you, dear old Daddy,
> I love you young or old.
> I would not trade you for a farm,
> Nor for a house of gold.
> You'r mine I'm yours, dear Daddy,
> Wherever we may be,
> And on this queer old planet
> You mean a lot to me

The second poem repeated the reframe, "Folks need a lot of loving. . ."

When she wrote her January letter to her father, Bibb had already begun to get things together for China. She cashed in a hundred and ten dollars worth of war bonds and was planning on how she would spend the one hundred and twenty five dollars that the Foreign Mission Board allowed them for supplies. She would be allowed to take three hundred and fifty pounds of goods with her.

Her last semester at the W.M.U. Training School was full of excitement. The renowned preacher George W. Truet came to Broadway Baptist Church for ten days of preaching in February. The well-known evangelist W. W, Hamilton came to campus to lecture for several weeks. There were friends like Frank Level, Miss Fleming, an ex-training school student, and one of Bibb's sister's friends from Shorter College, who dropped by. Life was anything but dull with one or two parties every week, including one for all the Mississippi girls. It was all very exciting.

The W.M.U. Training School was in downtown Louisville, Kentucky, and just a short distance from Southern Baptist Theological Seminary. Students from each school regularly saw each other. Romance was commonplace between the women at the Training School and men at the Seminary. I often have wondered how many young missionaries volunteered for their foreign assignments because they were in love or married to someone who was already committed to going overseas. Southern Seminary was ripe with missionary fervor. Professor George W. Carver was a leading missiologist, theologian, and biblical scholar at Southern Seminary. With Dr. Carvers teaching and the emphasis on missions at the W.M.U. Training School a very large group of young men and women were prepared and eager to go to their respective fields under the Southern Baptist Foreign Mission Board. Sixty missionaries were appointed in the summer of 1921 alone. Mary Bibb was one of them.

On May the second 1921 the Louisville Courier Journal published a picture of fifty young women who would graduate from the W.M.U. Training School that evening. It was the largest class of young women to finish the school up to that date. As I read over their names, I realized how many of them would go to China. Following graduation mother went to Tupelo to get ready to leave for the mission field.

Early in the summer of 1921 an interesting exchange took place between the pastors of the First Baptist Church of

Corinth, Mississippi, the Rev. C.W. Wright, and Bibb's pastor at the First Baptist Church in Tupelo, Alfred J. Dickinson, whom you will remember tried to discourage her from going to the mission field. The church in Corinth wanted to sponsor Mary Bibb and pay her salary, but Rev. Dickinson wrote back to the church in Corinth that the First Baptist Church in Tupelo had given a large sum of money to the Foreign Mission Board's $75,000,000 campaign, and it only seemed right that she be sponsored by the church in Tupelo. Dr. Ray of the Foreign Mission Board Secretary decided the issue in a letter to the church in Tupelo. Part of the gifts of the First Baptist Church would be used to pay Mary Bibb's salary that would be $800.00 a year. As they continued their gifts, they would be considered as her sponsor. He also reminded Rev. Dickinson that it actually took more than $800.00 to keep a missionary in the field. My Grandfather's offer to pay her salary was never brought up.

Bibb, as she was now called, already knew where she wanted to go. China! She and several other young women came under the influence of an old china hand, Miss Willy Kelly. Miss Kelly was a veteran missionary and a formidable person. She bore her self with dignity and authority. Although she was not tall, the way she stood, ramrod straight, made her appear dominating. There was a tilt to her head and a look in her eye that gave the appearance of superiority and, at times, even condescension. When I was a child, I found her intimidating and hated to have her eyes bore into mine through her wire-rimmed glasses. Like most women of her day, I am certain she was corseted. It kept her body in an appropriate shape for her station, but it also gave her a slight sense of belligerence. Miss Kelly used her furlough to travel from her Alabama home to neighboring states recruiting young women to do work among Chinese women. Her protégés were all young single women. When it became clear that the father of one of her recruits was adamantly opposed to his daughter going to China, Willy Kelly came to Tupelo to persuade my grandfather that mother should go. She guaranteed that she would personally look after my mother and her safety. How she planned to do the latter, I cannot imagine. She was not able to dissuade Judge Long that his daughter ought not to go. China was too far away and she would be gone too long. It took three to four weeks to cross the Pacific, and missionary furloughs to the U.S. were seven years apart. He would only change his mind later when it was inevitable.

As far as the family knew, until we recently found some old letters tucked away, my mother and father had not been particularly well acquainted in Louisville. However, we were wrong. They began corresponding during the summer. I found a letter written from Winder, Georgia written by my father on July 29. In the letter it is clear that he had written several times before and had gotten only one reply in which my mother had addressed him as "Dear Sir". He teased back by addressing his letter, "Dear Madam." Both of them seemed exceptionally busy preparing to leave.

Mother's entire family, except her sister Julia and her husband, Dan, gathered at 543 Jefferson St. for her departure. On Saturday August 20th everyone posed together on the front porch around my mother who was seated in the center in a rocking chair. Some of the neighbors were there, as was mother's close friend Pearl Guyton. It was a time of deep feelings and sweet sadness. By then my grandfather had given his consent for mother to go. But the tug on everyone's heart was mirrored in the expressions on their faces.

Bibb left Tupelo with Miss Kelly, who later confided in her that she felt like kissing the Judge when they departed late Sunday afternoon. The next day Bibb mailed a card to her mother from St. Louis. She had lost her training school pin in the lavatory basis, but it had been retrieved by the conductor. She had also lost her briefcase key, but found it too. She wrote, ". . . am holding on with a death grip to my other possessions and life." The next day she arrived in Chicago and sent off another post card that she had written on the train. The third day she posted a card from Minneapolis saying all was well. The next days were spent on board the train, The Olympian, as the group made its way across the Midwest and Northwest, through flat lands, a dust storm, and finally the mountains. It was on this leg of the trip that mother began to keep a dairy of sorts. Two cards came from Seattle before they sailed. In one she said that all of her baggage had arrived and that she had gotten her visa at the Japanese consulate and was prepared to leave. The last card she lost before she could mail it, and a stranger picked it up in the McDougall-Gauthenick Department store and mailed it for her.

Seattle was exciting. The Seattle Star, newspaper, feature a picture of the departing group of missionaries and singled out Miss Mary Bibb Long and Mrs. U. W. Level with individual pictures and short biographies. Writing to her mother Bibb described herself in the picture as looking "positively frightful. . .look like a criminal." The Y.M.C.A. in Seattle had a tea for the group sponsored by Mrs. Weyerhaeuser and a number of the party toured different parts of the city.

Back in the capital of Mississippi, Jackson, on Sunday August 28th, the day after Bibb and the others sailed from Seattle on the Hawkeye State the leading Mississippi newspaper, The Daily Clarion-Ledger, also carried an article on the large number of Southern Baptist Missionaries who were leaving for foreign fields. Bibb and her friends Winnie Bennett of Hattisburg, Ullin Leavell of Oxford, and Wm. Ellison Allen of Amory (who was going to Brazil) were featured on the front page. Several other papers across the south listed the members of the group. A Richmond, Virginia paper listed the names of the group by states. Another regional paper noted that Bibb had made a name for herself in Mississippi, particularly with her association with the young women at Blue Mountain College.

With great fanfare, the sounds of "Farewell to Thee" by the band, and some tears, Mother, and her fellow travelers, sailed the last of August from Seattle on the maiden transpacific voyage of the Admiral Line's S.S. Hawkeye State with about fifty other missionaries and their children bound for Japan and China. Mrs. Lea, a family friend gave mother a goodbye kiss for the General, and she and her sons waved farewell from the pier. Some of the missionaries were returning from furlough, but the vast majority were new appointees, many of them single. The first days sailing up Puget Sounds was smooth, but the initial days out on the Pacific the ship rolled with the waves, and Bibb was seasick. The third day found her out of her cabin and lying flat on a deck chair. On Sunday in spite of the roll of the ship, with as many missionaries as there were aboard, services were held both morning and evening. Dr McDaniel, an older Baptist missionary from Soochow, China had the morning service; and, Dr. Fisher of the Presbyterian Board presided over the evening worship. Already, denominational differences where beginning to fade into the background.

Sitting up to write was a chore that she didn't attempt until the fifth day, Wednesday. Monday she had spoken at some length with Mr. Ware, as she still called him. The next week when the sailing turned rough again, Bibb and her friends were back in the deck chairs. She wrote, "Mr. Ware brought or rather had our dinner sent up to us, peeled our fruit and was nurse generally until he was tuck down too." As they neared the Aleusian Island the weather turned worse. As Bibb described it, she enjoyed the storm. ". . .we enjoyed seeing the boat mount up on the waves, ride there, and come down, sometimes the propeller was out of the water. Then there was a terrible bump when it struck in again. The waves broke over the top deck and the spray was beautiful. . . last night we saw phosphor in the waves; it makes a beautiful, dull light." After the storm the sea flattened out, and life returned to near normal.

It is not clear how her relationship with "Mr. Ware" was going. She told her mother to tell Mrs. Berry and Mrs. Thomas that things were going ". . . so far so good, but my fingers are on my pulse, for there are many peaches in Georgia." For most of the passengers the trip turned out to be very congenial. The group was exceptional talented, and on the evening of September fifth the ship's Captain arranged an evening of music with the ship's band, Prince Jack's Hawaiian Jazz Band, and some ten musical numbers by passengers. The printed program for the evening indicated that the group was in high spirits. Prince Jack's Band ended the program with John Phillip Susa's <u>Stars and Stripes Forever</u>.

Their first port was Yokohama, and they took the opportunity to shop and see the sights. Bibb was a bit taken back by the lack of cloths that some Japanese men wore at home and their home workshops. Nevertheless, she, Rose Marlow, the Wisenhunts and Mr. Ware went by electric train on a trip to Tokyo and visited the Imperial Palace, the Imperial Museum, Imperial University, Tibya Park, several Buddhist Temples, and the largest department store. Kobe, the next stop, was equally interesting. They visited the first Baptist Church to be established in Japan, although they missed the worship service.

In Kobe the missionaries who were going to North China (Misses Bennett, Grayson, and Smith, and Messer Ware and Pruitt) left the ship. Bibb's only comment was that she hoped to see them again sometime.

My mother and father had known each other in Louisville while they were in school, but they had never dated or spent much time together. On the S.S. Hawkeye they not only got to know each other better, but fell in love. It seems that my father already had strong feelings for my mother. Mother' s feeling were not so clear. There was a problem, however. My father was appointed to mission work in Whangshien, North China, and would go on to Peking (as it was then called) for Mandarin language school, while Mother would continue to Shanghai where she had been appointed to do evangelistic work at Old North Gate Church, the training place for many of Willy Kelly's minions. She would learn Shanghai or Wu dialect. From mother's side it would be up to Miss Kelly to guide the relationship. The older married missionaries aboard ship let it be know that they did not what a single, single man to leave the ship; they gave both parties very strong encouragement. In fact Bibb was to write to her mother that it would have been embracing at times if she and Mr. Ware had not had an understanding. Two days before she arrived in Shanghai, Bibb wrote a private letter to her mother and father that told them that Mr. Ware had indeed told her that he loved her, though she had already drawn the conclusion for his actions and looks. They were considering getting married in November after they had been alone and had time to think about it. The problem of their assignments to Shanghai and Whangshien would have to be worked out, and the question of studying two different dialects of Chinese had to be dealt with. Shanghai would need another evangelistic missionary in a year and a half when Miss Priest would leave on furlough. However, the work in Whangshien would be starting an Institutional Ministry that had great promise. Both parties were willing to do whatever God wanted and the Foreign Mission Board decided. Dr. Ray, the head of the Foreign Mission Board would be in China shortly, and could make the decision. Miss Kelly was for Mr. Ware's move to Shanghai, and Bibb relied on her heavily.

In the letter Bibb gave her parents Mr. Ware's history. She seemed to have been particularly impressed that he had grown up without the good fortune that she had ". . . in having a loving tender, sympathetic mother, rather makes me love him the more." His ideals were as high as hers and there was ". . . not an ounce of conceit in him- I'd like him better if there were more." She described him: "He is not handsome, tho not ugly. . . . Laughingly he refers to himself as bow legged and slough-footed, but he is rather unjust. Any way I'm not thinking of marrying him for looks." They had agreed that were they to marry they would begin each day with a devotional time together. On a lighter note she states: ". . . it goes without saying that he does not smoke, chew, drink, and the like. I think he is typical of Papa's ideal preacher. I've never heard him preach and he has never held a pastorate- but he gave me an outline of a sermon and if that is typical, he's alright." In the rest of the letter she tells more details about his family and asks her parents, "What is your pleasure?" Actually Miss Kelly would be the one to work out the problems and details.

A letter from the Foreign Mission Board written on the fourteenth of September notified the Longs in Tupelo that a cable had been received from Shanghai saying that Bibb had arrived safely. It was followed by a letter from Bibb begun on the fourteenth and completed a few days later. The Hawkeye State had tied up at one of the floating jetties on the Whangpoo River that flows into the mouth of the Yangtse River, and upstream forms the waterfront in Shanghai. The floating jetties were necessary because the channel of the river does not run along the shore, and it was necessary to build the jetties some fifty yards or so from the bank and tie them to the peers along the bank with floating causeways. The ship was met by numerous missionaries and their families from as far away as Soochow. Among them were people who would be life long friends: Miss Priest, Miss Lyne, the Steels, and Mr. Jacksons, The reception was warm and festive; people waved to each other from the jetties to the boat and those on the boat waved back.

As soon as they had cleared customs Miss Kelly and Bibb got their baggage together and proceeded by automobile to 466 Rue La Fayette, which was to be home for the next few years. The Rue La Fayette compound and most of it furnishings had been given to Miss Kelly by Mathew T. Yates' daughter, Mrs. Seaman, who was married to a very successful business man in Shanghai and was quite wealthy. Bibb and Miss Kelly were joined by Miss Priest, Edith Whisenhunt, and Miss McMimm for a dinner of soup, beef-loaf, potatoes, rice, butter beans, apricots and cake. It was not what the new missionaries had imagined. After dinner they went to Eliza Yates girl's school and met with the missionaries there.

Miss Kelly was the ranking leader of the Women's Missionary Union in Shanghai. She was also the senior missionary at Old North Gate Baptist Church, the first Baptist Church to be founded in Shanghai. She was extremely influential in the Shanghai Mission at every level. Willy Kelly and Miss Priest presided over their young women from a compound built in the French Concession. You entered the compound through a long archway built through a building on Rue Lafayette. When you entered the compound, beautiful flowerbeds, and a vegetable garden immediately surrounded you. The short road circled a flowerbed at the entrances of the two buildings that made up the living quarters for the young women and a few young couples. There was nothing remotely primitive about the place. When a young women stepped off the ship in Shanghai and was driven in an automobile to the Rue Lafayette compound, she was transported to very modern and attractive home. She was immediately reassured. A large three-story brick stucco house was the living areas for Miss Kelly's and Miss Priest's protégés. The second building was a girl's school. On each floor across the front of the residential building were long open-air porches.

The compound was completely surrounded by other building and hidden from them behind a tall woven bamboo fence and trees. But it was here that many decisions were made about the lives of the young women who would serve the W.M.U. in China. This was mother's first home in China. Although at this point in time a married man and his wife might be in residence on the W.M.U. compound for a short period of time, it eventually became a tightly knit group of single women who had their permanent residence there. They were mother's closest friends. Later on they all became my courtesy aunts, and I will have to admit I enjoyed an inordinate amount of attention from them.

Miss Kelly was a remarkable woman. Old North Gate Church was the first Baptist Church in Shanghai. It was almost one hundred years old when mother was first appointed there. In the 1924 annual North Gate report Miss Kelly states that the church is well on its way to being self-supporting, self-governing, and self-propagating. This is remarkable because it is precisely the underlying principles of the Three Self Church, the officially recognized Church in China today. Here were articulated in 1924 the aims and goals of the present official Church in China long before the formation of the Three Self Movement during the communist period.

Mother immediately hit it off well with Miss Priest and the two of them worked out her assignments at the school at Old North Gate. Although Bibb did not speak any Chinese she was to supervise three Chinese teachers who taught kindergarten and primary school. Mother's description of Miss Priest was, "She is tall, has beautiful eyes that are so jolly, a keen sense of humor and is so loving and lovable."

The next few day included an orientation to the other mission work in Shanghai. The joint venture of Northern and Southern Baptist, the University of Shanghai, or as it was known in Chinese, The Wu Dialect University, was a big campus spread out along the Whangpoo River down stream for the city. It was already well populated with students registering for the new term. The sixteenth was mother's first day to spend time by her self. The tone of her letter on that day bordered on homesickness, but she bravely described the little old lady she had seen with bound feet and the few men who still wore cues. Both were technically illegal under the laws of the new Chinese Republic. Cues had been a sign of loyalty to the Ching Dynasty, but many laboring class Chinese men simply wore them out of custom. Given her sense of modesty, she was having some difficulty with seeing Chinese men stripped to the waist while they worked and urinating whereever it was convenient. But she loved the way that young Chinese girls cut their hair in bangs across their foreheads. In a letter to Olivia she told her younger sister about Chinese social customs and funeral arrangements. She also encouraged her younger sister to study hard and come to China when she graduated to teach the skills she was learning in theater.

As were many young missionaries arriving in China at the time, she was appalled at he poverty and unhealthy condition that many people lived in. Old North Gate Church was just about a mile away from the Rue La Fayette compound, and a walk to the church really did expose one to the working poor. It was hard for her to take in that so many children were going without schooling, and she lamented that the school at Old North Gate could not serve them because the school was self supporting and most of the children could not have paid the tuition. Whenever they rode anywhere in the car and stopped for whatever reason, they always drew a crowd of curious people around them.

On the twenty second of September she received her first letter from home. She had gotten three letters from Kobe, but had not heard from the "North China" group since they had gotten to China. A letter had already been sent to Dr. Ray apprising him of Miss Long's and Mr. Ware's desires. Mail service in Shanghai to the United States was publicized several days before a ship would leave for the United States and people would write letters like mad to make the next announced boat. When mail arrived it too was publicized and the actual number of mailbags delivered by a given ship was published. It often took several days for letters and packages to be sorted before they reached their intended destination. Letters sent back to the United States bore U.S., not Chinese, stamps and postmarks. Sometimes the post mark would be the name of the ship carrying the letter, and at other time it would be the post office of the port in the U.S. where he ship unloaded its mail.

It was on the twenty second of September that she went with some of the others and registered at the American Consulate, thinking that this would make her safe while she was in China. During the previous twelve months more than 3000 Americans had registered in Shanghai. Bibb also opened a bank account at the American Oriental Bank. Not everything was serious work. She and Mr. Jackson went over to Eliza Yates Girl's School and played tennis with Rose Marlow and Miss Larrett. Then they all took the tram as far as it would take them to the edge of town and had their first rickshaw ride back home.

By the end of the second week Bibb seem to be acclimated to her new surroundings. On Saturday Miss Kelly, she, and the Wisenhunts were welcomed into Old North Church by the congregation in an elaborate ceremony. Of course the major part of the ceremony honored Miss Kelly. But her place was now established, and she was becoming accustomed to her surroundings. Sunday after morning worship at Old North Gate, a group of the missionaries went for an evening service at the Community Church where services were in English, and ties were made with missionaries, and business people who were all expatriates. This seemed to close the circle and complete with satisfaction her acceptance of her new life in Shanghai, China.

Back in Tupelo, Olivia came home and immediately set out for New York and John Murray Anderson's School for actors. She was determined to be an actress and to get on stage. Of course this mean she had to learn to dance as well, so she enrolled in Martha Graham's dance school under the tutelage of Sonia Serova.

CHAPTER THREE

Hamp and Mary Bibb

Both Hamp's and Mary Bibb's correspondence in the first few weeks of their arrival in China gives very little indication that they knew very much about the social turmoil that they were entering. Unlike missionaries of today, they had almost no orientation to the country where they were assigned. Within the first two weeks Bibb wrote several observations to her mother about Chinese life. She tells about a Chinese funeral in detail as though it were her first knowledge of Chinese customs. Hamp's description of the orphans in Pingtu indicates that he had little knowledge of the great famine that spread across North China in the 1920 and 1921 as a result of the great drought in 1919. Neither of them was politically aware of the intrigue that was taking place around them. Of course there were good reasons for their lack of knowledge. They did not have the advantages that we have of instant televised news from around the world. In fact there were very few correspondences covering China whose information got back to the American public. The principal players on the Chinese scene were so numerous and dispersed that it was difficult for those who made it there business to know what was going on, to keep up with the daily changes and even definitive events. Probably the most important fact was that many missionaries during this period were not interested in politics or the culture traumas of the countries to which they were assigned. They were idealists who, having felt the call of God, went out into an needy and unfriendly world to heal, educate, and above all spread the good news of God's love by their actions and their words.

In the tidal flux that was washing over China, there were three major crosscurrents which were very different, but were tied together by events and critical players. The flow was washing away all the recognizable boundary markers of the past and carrying derby to every crevice of the countryside. The first swirl of untamed emerging events was political instability and change. The second transforming force was the cacophony of voices advocating new and often radical ideas. The third unrelenting driving force was the rise of an economic and technological innovations and growth. Into these three power generating, muddy, rivers there were language and ethnic differences, provincial loyalties, urban and rural conflicts, industrial and farming inequities, educated elites and uneducated masses struggling for a place. Many people struggled just to survive. Others struggled for power. Some struggled for quiet and hope. If there was one common denominator, it was to be rid of the strangle hold of foreign powers and to be a nation equal in status with the other great peoples of the world. All of these forces, these energies, were elbowing one another, coming together without boundaries or controls.

In a country that is undergoing the demise of its traditions and gods, people look for new values, traditions, and religions. A "twilight of the gods" leaves a gapping hold in a society that sucks new religions and ideologies in like a great whirlpool. After World War II this was quite evident in Korean and Japanese cultures where hundreds of new religions sprung up around charismatic leaders. Often the new religious traditions were a hi-bred between the past and the present. Sometimes they had completely foreign roots and grounding. Many times they were eschatological, and messianic, promising a great future of prosperity and peace. Being a missionary in China after the fall of the Ching Dynasty was to live, teach, and preach in culture that was hungry to achieve a new identity and set of value. It was a plowed field waiting to be planted.

Bibb disembarked in Shanghai on September fourteenth, and Hamp landed in Qingdao on the eighteenth. Both of them were in China less than a month before the tenth anniversary of the Double Tenth, October 10th, the date in 1911 recognized as the anniversary of the fall of the Ching Dynasty and the rise of the Republic of China. Between 1906 and 1911 there had been six unsuccessful attempts to over through the Ching Dynasty. The final revolution against the Manchu or Ching Dynastry began in the city of Wuchang, but took several months to be completed. Sun Yat-sen, the father of the revolutionary movement was not in China at this time. He was in the United States where he read about the events in a Denver newspaper. Sun made his way back to China through Europe, getting the blessings of the French and British and their support against Japan's aid to the Emperor. Sun arrived in China December twelfth. Within four days, the provincial delegates elected him the Provisional President of the new Republic. The capital would be Nanking, both because it was in Central China, which was more easily accessible to delegates from around the country, and it was much less apt to be attacked by foreign forces that were concentrated along the coasts.

The Ching court had not yet abdicated, and it attempted to persuade Yuan Shih-kai, the most powerful military person in China at the time, to take the imperial side. Yuan, had no love for the Ching, and was also courted by the revolutionaries who felt that a strong military leader was necessary to keep the country together and in order. The Revolutionaries consequently promised him the presidency of the Republic if he would force the Ching out of office. Sun Yat-sin pragmatically committed himself to being the Provisional President if Yuan would take the Regular Presidency. Yuan and other military leaders persuaded the Manchu princes that time had run out for them. Sun then set the conditions for the transfer of the Presidency to Yuan. First, Yuan would notify the foreign ministers and consulates of the Ching's abdication. Second, Yuan would publicly give his support to the Republic. Sun would resign when he was notified of the abdication by the foreign diplomatic and consular corps. Fourth, the parliament would elect Yuan as Provisional President; and finally, Yuan would pledge to honor the constitution to be prepared by the representative parliament; and, until he did so, he would have no military power.[i]

On February twelfth 1912 the Ching abdicated, and Yuan pledged his support to the Republic. Sun resigned the provisional presidency the next day and put Yuan's name forward as the new provisional President, and on the fourteenth of February the provisional parliament elected Yuan as Provisional President. According to the agreement Yuan was to come to Nanking to head the new government, but he refused to leave his power base in the North and remained in Peking. He was inaugurated there on March tenth, and the following day a Provisional Constitution was published. Sun formally resigned on April the first and the parliament made Peking the capital four days later. Thus began the revolution.

These days that brought so much promise were the beginning of bitter internal bickering and treachery. Yuan by appointing his cronies, by assassination, and by intimidation of the Parliament soon exercised control and out maneuvered the various political parties and cliques that had evolved in the Parliament. In 1914 he called a second constitutional convention that made him essentially the new monarch, but without that title. China was vulnerable and foreign governments were not hesitant to take advantage, the Japanese in particular made twenty-one demands of the new government. Yuan yielded to the Japanese humiliating demands; signed agreements with Britain and Russia to recognize their special interests in China; and encourage internal movements to return to a monarchy. Sun, who had fled to Japan for his life, began a counter movement. Provinces began to break away from the Peking government, and Yuan's own cronies seemed to back away from him before his inauguration. Then suddenly, on June sixth 1916, Yuan died. What followed was a long period of warlord rulers whose control over their parts of China would ebb and flow. The warlords fought and ruled their respective areas from 1916-27. In 1917 an attempt was made to restore the Ching emperor, Pu-yi, but it lasted only twelve days. This was followed by the ascendancy over the forces around Peking of a powerful warlord Duan Chi-jui,. Because he controlled Beijing, Duan was considered by the outside world as the representative of China as a whole. World War II had begun, and Duan used China's entry into the war on the side of the Allies in April 1917 as a pretext to gain foreign favor and to illegally borrow large sums of money from the Japanese. Officially the Chinese government entered World War I on the allied side, but it was not a decision made by a unified government. The five major warlords who ruled their separate provinces with more or less power were not parties to China's entry into the war. Although Duan formally spoke for the nation as a whole, he did not govern the majority of the country. In the south Sun was trying to rally the anti-imperial, anti-warlord generals, and leaders to try to restore a constitutional republic. The sea-sawing back and forth of warlord's power and the general chaos which descended on China was to last well past the time Hamp and Mary Bibb arrived in China. The political reunification of China would begin in 1922 under the leadership of one of Sun's protégés Chiang Kai-shek, But it would not be completed until 1926 after Sun's death on March 12, 1925.

The internal political and military confrontations masked other events that were occurring. The Republic had not ended the concessions and extra-territoriality rights of the foreign colonial powers in China. Foreign powers kept the ports that they had been granted under treaties with the Manchu's. They continued to exploit one-sided trade agreements, and the removal of foreigners from the jurisdiction of Chinese law. Japan annexed Taiwan and

Korea, which was a Chinese client state, with impunity. Britain, France, The United States, Japan, Germany, Italy, Russia and Portugal all maintained their claims and positions. All of the colonial powers tried to influence the decisions of the Peking government. Consequently there was great resentment and disillusionment among the Chinese population. This resentment broke into the open on May Fourth 1919 with a national reaction that crossed the jurisdictions of the warlords.

Chinese had been going overseas for work and education for decades. One of the great incentives of the Republican revolutaries was to bring China in the modern world on an equal footing with the great powers. Because of the manpower shortage in France and Britain during World War I, the French recruited over 96,000 Chinese to do menial work both in the war effort and in French daily life. A German U-boat sank the first boatload of 543 Chinese on their way to France in the Mediterranean Sea. In addition some 2000 died in France. Many of the others returned to China when they had made enough money to come back and start a life above the prevailing poverty. China had been persuaded to enter World War I on the side of the Allies with the informal understanding that the Japanese would not take over the concessions granted the Germans by the Ching Dynasty. Chinese had been going overseas for work and education for decades. One of the great incentives of the Republican revolutionaries was to bring China in the modern world on an equal footing with the great powers. When the war ended there were parades in Peking and high expectations throughout the country. But when the Chinese diplomats went to Versailles in 1919, they discovered that they had been betrayed as early as 1917 by Duan who had made a secret treaty with the Japanese that gave them control over the area that the Germans had held and indenture most of the railroad through Shandong Province. The great powers at Versailles (including the U.S.) upheld the legality of the treaty with Japan.

When the news arrived in China, it provoked a student protest in Peking on May the fourth. Mass protests by students and workers throughout the country followed. The Chinese diplomats at Versailles were instructed not to sign the treaty. Even if they had desired to do so, they were forcibly prevented from leaving their hotels to attend the signing by Chinese students and demonstrators. In Peking students from thirteen colleges and universities demonstrated against the Versailles Treaty. They gathered in Teinanmen Square and vowed to form a union to awaken the masses. Then they marched some three thousand strong toward the foreign legations, only to be turned back by foreign guards and the Chinese police. One student was killed and thirty-two arrested. Student demonstrations and mass popular protests followed throughout the country. A transforming moment had occurred. China was ripe for a new ideology, and May Fourth would be the catalyst to bring in a new era of intellectual as well as political change. Students began reading widely in Western literature and political theory. Confucianism was now an anachronism to be replaced by a new understanding of life which would included the masses. Everything intellectual was up for grabs. Out of the May Fourth Movement would come the new intellectual leaders Cai Yuan-pei, Chen Du-xiu, and Hu Shi. John Dewey would teach in China in 1919-1920; Bertram Russell in 1920- 21; Margaret Sanger 1922. Even Albert Einstein would visit in 1922. New political movements informed by Western technology and ideology would spring up throughout the country. Students like Chou En-lai and Deng Xiao Ping would go to France on a work-study program in 1919-20. Mao Tse-tung was already discussing Communism with his friends in Beijing and Shanghai. In Shanghai one month before Bibb arrived (July 1921) the first plenary meeting of the Chinese Communist Party was held.

The political and intellectual changes in China occurred in the shadow of a colossal change in economic and technical development. Foreign investment skyrocketed, as did the activities of Chinese entrepreneurs. Railroads made travel back and forth between North and South China as easy as the old river system had made China's East and West accessible to one another. Mining, textiles, tobacco, and modern advertising came to full bloom overnight, as did labor unions and banking. Shanghai would be the new center of commerce, rivaled only by Hong Honk. The third strand of tidal change has no marked date for its beginning; it simply explodes, first on the coasts and then inland. It is in this world that Hamp and Bibb will have to choose where they will work and live. Their choice depended on the Foreign Mission Board's and their colleagues' approval.

On September 25 when Hamp reached Whangshien where he had been appointed to work there was a letters from Bibb to which he had so anxiously looked forward. However, included in the letters to him, Bibb had enclosed a copy of a letter she had written to Dr. Ray the Secretary of the Foreign Mission Board. Among Bibb's letters there is a partial, pencil written copy of the letter she wrote to Dr. Ray. Whether it was the one she mailed to Dr Ray and to Hamp is not clear. She began by saying to Ray that he will understand; then tells him that she and Mr. Ware would like to work together rather than separately in Shanghai and Hwangshien. They have not set a date for a wedding and would not set one without his advice and consent. "What is your pleasure?" There is a need to know because he will be learning Mandarin and she will be learning Shanghai dialect during the coming year, and for the sake of the work a decision needed to be made soon. She tells him that they have already agreed between themselves that either one of them would change their assignment to where the needs were the greatest, of course with his consent.

What was disturbing to Hamp was what followed: "I want him to come to Shanghai, and there are several reasons. One is Miss Priest needs me now to help her in the kindergarten and primary departments of the S.S. and school. 2nd, when Miss Priest goes home on furlough year after next, there should be someone here to take the school work. . . Again, you will remember I asked to come to Central or Interior China because of the climate. I am very cold natured and might freeze up North. Fourth, his work as assigned is general evangelistic work and mine is more special work. . ." She continues her argument by saying that there is no one else who wants to do the work she is doing and there are evangelistic opportunities for Mr. Ware to train the three Chinese who will be serving the eight out stations. He is particularly suited for this work because of his unassuming and modest nature and his ability to take the initiative.

Hamp wrote Bibb in reply,

> "While your letter, breathing your presence in every line, gave me great joy, yet it was impossible

not to read some things that are very clear. It is clear that your heart goes out to the work there in Shanghai and that you feel your responsibilities and obligations to the station there. I have been tying to make myself say, 'I'm glad' – it has been hard to do because of what it means. If your love for Shanghai were like your love for your mother, (permanent and ever warm - but not holding you back) I think I could say it with ease. I have been trying to say it any way as you seem to be uncertain as to the will of the Master. If <u>you</u> tell me plainly it is the will of the Master that you work in Shanghai, I will say it."

Hamp had also written Dr. Ray, as he and Bibb's had agreed, but it was a very different kind of letter. As he put it, it was "light and gay" because he thought he already knew what Dr. Ray would say. The mission field was still a man's domain, and Ray would want Bibb to join him in Hwanghsien. One of the agreements that they had made that last night on the Hawkeye, though Hamp had resisted it, was that they would both be willing to leave their work to be assigned with the other. In his letter he admits that his reluctance had been due to what his fellow men workers would say if he left his appointment to go to Shanghai to be with her. Things didn't work that way on the mission field. It had always been that men invited women to join them in their work, and Hamp was sure that this would be Dr. Ray's decision. It seems that even Miss Kelly had plainly expressed that opinion while they were aboard ship; and, "Some of my friends consider it a joke that I should even think of such a thing." Questioning her reaction he asks, "What would she think of him now? Struggling over custom, when the girl he loved was at stake?" Thinking back over their agreement, he is not sure whether or not he has been fair with her when they made the agreement, because he assumed the outcome would be that she would join him. Dr. Ray, being a man, would take a man's point-of-view. However, he writes,

> I would not have you come for the world simply because of Dr. Ray's word. If you come, I want you to come because you believe it in accordance with the Master's will and because your heart tells you your greatest joy and peace of mind would be here. Unless you can see a greater opportunity for the exercise of your powers under God's guidance, a richer and fuller life, here than there, then, I think you ought not to come. Although I am writing this to you, I am saying the same thing to myself, believing that your own conscience approves. I realize that coming here means for you to give up many things and take upon yourself some awful responsibilities. I realize there are hardships to be endured and I refuse to paint it otherwise. It is because I realize these things that I refuse to insist in your coming. It is for you – not some one else - to make the decision. If you feel under obligation to remain there this year until some one else comes to relieve you, I shall not complain.

He signs the letter, "Sincerely yours (without rivals?)", Hamp Ware.

Between September the twenty sixth and October the first there seems to have been a number of letters written by each of them to one another. His letters are the only ones that were kept. Hamp's October first letter chided Bibb for miscounting his letters; he had written six or more and only received two. Before he responded to what she had written he told her that he would be leaving for Peking either that day or the next. His baggage, which he had left at the Chinese inn on the way to Hwangshien, had been slow to catch up with him, and he had missed the first boat to Peking. This would put him a day late for the beginning of language school. He was stuffed with food. The Hwangshein missionaries and Chinese church leaders had held numerous dinners, teas, and receptions for them. There were over five hundred students at the reception given by the teachers from the mission schools. What impressed him the most was the way in which the teachers, both men and women, worked together so democratically with a brotherly spirit.

The second half of the letter is written in reply to Bibb's questions concerning their relationship. Hamp writes:

> Bibb you ask me if there is any reason why you should not trust yourself, you life and happiness, to me. The line before that you said, 'all I ask is you whole-hearted love.' . . .Somehow, though, I am a little too practical and prosaic to believe that that is all that you will need for life and happiness. Do you think that the man who gets drunk and treats his wife mean while he is drunk, does not love her? I know he does love her. Bibb, the biggest thing in the way of your trusting yourself to me is me myself. You have had a slight taste of my stubbornness, and you have heard something about how I dislike conveniences. You have also see a

spark of my quick temper. . . I <u>do</u> wonder that you can see things in me to love. . . Why you should give up your work to join me in making a home is more than I can answer. I am just hoping that it is not all a dream.

This letter ends, "Sincerely Yours, Hamp Ware."

Hamp's next letter was mailed from Peking on October fourth. By this time they had agreed that they would set aside time each morning to be "together in the spirit." Bibb's letters that were waiting for him in Peking, kept his mind on her as he unpacked. As he wrote, he tells her not to worry about presuming too much on him. Say what she wanted to say. Since she had ask what he wanted, he wanted her to come to come to Peking to language school as soon as possible. That was why he had spoken so spiritedly on the Hawkeye. If she were not ready for marriage, then come on anyway; that could be settled later. He refused to set a date for her to come and left it up to her, even though the thought of her being there near by was extremely strong. To give wait to his argument he told her that he had talked with Miss Caldwell, and she and the others thought that this was the practical thing to do. Nevertheless the choice was hers, and he hoped that she would tell him what was on her mind. The coolness of the previous letter was replaced by, "Honest to goodness, I wish I could kiss you 'good night' tonight. May I? Goodnight. Hamp Ware."

Two days later Hamp writes a newsy letter about all of the Southern Baptist Missionaries who were there in Peking and particularly those who were in language school. They all had places to stay now and were settling in. Misses

Humphrey, Bennett, and Dr. and Mrs. Gaston were staying at the same hostile where he was, about fifteen minuets for the school. Misses Greyson and Kiethey were staying with the Andersons at the language school. Misses Barritt, Stribling, and Alexander are staying with the Puitt's. One of the older missionaries couples, the Herrings, were returning to Pingtu. He was beginning to find his way around and in the process had found out how to get his hair cut. It seems that Miss Smith had warned them about eating Chinese food outside the mission homes, but Emmitt Ayer and Miss Watson had taken them out for a big meal and they had enjoyed it. Mr. Lawton and Dr. Ayers had already issued them and invitation to come to Hwangshien for the Christmas holidays. Dr. Ayers wanted to know if he could make reservations for them to go to Chefoo for the summer vacation. He had not replied to either invitation and remarked, "They sure do take care of your out here, don't they?" The last paragraph of the letter tells her how much he enjoys reading her letters before he goes to bed. It's just like a visit, even though it is not by moonlight. This letter ends with, "Love from Hamp."

If Hamp is being treated royally in Peking, Bibb is being treated equally well in Shanghai. In a long letter to her mother begun on October the eighth, she told in great detail of going to an all day affair and feast given by a son of a Chinese official in his father's memory. This would be her first use of chopsticks. The son, Mr. Zau, and his entire family, were members of Old North Gate Church. She had visited the son's gardens several days before, and they were beautiful. During the week she and Miss Priest had gone to hear Dr. R.A. Torry, the noted theologian and biblical scholar, preach. But, the highlight of the week was the receipt of a number of letters from home that she compared to. . ." amalgamation cake, ambrosia, ice cream, fruit cocktail, a turkey course, and pineapple-banana salad with cherries. . ." As she put it, "You would have to be on the field and wait over Sunday after a boat has come in on Saturday and then wait until afternoon Monday to appreciate a new missionary's feelings when she's had only one letter from home." Much of this disconnected twelve-page letter is interspersed with comments about her family and responses to the news from home. At times she is homesick, but sitting down to write a letter to a member of the family puts her at home as though she were in a conversation with at home with them. She is still concerned about her Papa's health and happiness. She had already bought Christmas gifts when she stopped off in Japan and would have them in the mail soon. Language school had already begun, and she gave her mother a lesson in the pictorial nature of Chinese' characters. Bibb seemed to have taken good care of her health. Growing up I had never thought of my mother as being athletically inclined. However, she speaks of walking around the city, playing tennis, and visiting the gym at Old North Gate Church to play basketball.

The letter indicated clearly that Bibb was struck by the commitment of the Chinese Christians that she has met or heard about in Old Northgate Church. How much this influenced her desire to stay in Shanghai is difficult to determine. The letter to her mother ends with a remarkable story told to her by Miss Kelly about her mentor's old bible-women, "Zung Ta Ta," (sic). According to Miss Kelly, Zung Ta Ta was orphaned at a very young age and sold as a young girl to a brothel where she stayed until she was seventeen. She prayed to her Chinese deities to be saved from the situation and was eventually bought by a wealthy Chinese gentleman to be his concubine. The gentleman's Big Wife hated her and was cruel to her. She was jealous of her because the younger women had cut out a part of her arm in appreciation to the gentleman when he was sick, and had made a soup to heal him. Over the next few years as his concubine, she had two sons and a daughter by him. The Big Wife had no children. When Zung Ta Ta's daughter died, she was very depressed and would go to her temple to pray. One day, while riding in a rickshaw by a church, she heard the Christian gospel being preached and began secretly attending. In a month's time she wanted to join the church. She discovered that her husband had been secretly interested as well. They asked for membership, but were told by Dr. Mathew T. Yates, who was the pastor of the church, that in a Christian church a person could have only one wife. Mr. Zung then put away his first wife, because under Chinese custom he could not put away the mother of his children. They were then accepted into the church. Both Mr. Zung and Zung Tai Tai continued to send money to the ex-Big Wife, but she would have nothing to do with them and only accepted the money through a third party. On her deathbed ex-Big Wife sent for Zung Tai Tai to ask her for her forgiveness for not acknowledging her gifts. She had not only accepted the money, but had read the messages in which the money had been wrapped. Zung Tai Tai told her that she did not blame her; it was she who had taken her husband away from her. Big Wife replied that because of Zung Tai Tai's exemplary life, she had come to follow Zung Tai Tai's god; and when she died she would go to be with Zung Tai Tai's god. Getting to know the dedication of the Chinese Christians around Old North Gate Church had a profound impact on Bibb.

The letters between Hamp and Bibb often reflected what the other person wrote several days before and had since changed their mind. Hamp's October the tenth letter from Peking addresses questions about their relationship that Bibb had put to him that she had earlier had on her mind. But judging from what she wrote to her mother, she seemed to have already gone beyond those issues. Initially Bibb had taken some of the things Hamp had written in his earlier letters as "curckleburrs." He had received her reply to these letters and wanted to take some of the sting out of what she had perceived him as saying, especially about what other people would think of him if he went to Shanghai. However, she had already written in the letter to her mother begun on October the eighth, that she had planned to go to Soochow for the week, but was not going because she was thinking about going to Peking. "I'm most sure I'll go but I'll have a few more days in which to decide and write so I'll wait." The long letter was written over a period of five days. In the early part of the letter she continues her positive attitude toward going to Peking by stating that among the items, which she had brought from Tupelo, was a small can of fig preserves, which she tells her mother that she plans to keep until she starts housekeeping. Bibb wrote, "I laugh when I think of what we will start with, five plates, dessert at that, six orange spoons & three others, and a vase, two beds and a heater. But we aren't going to start soon, that is in a year, don't think we will marry before next summer. Miss K. & P want us to have it (the wedding) here even if we live in Hwangshien." In the margin she gives her mother instructions that this letter is not to be put in her dairy, nor is the information to be shared outside the family. Several days pass and she adds to the letter that Hamp has written and is extremely anxious for her to come on to language school and that she will probably leave for Peking on Thursday with Mrs. Johnson from the college in Shanghai. Hedging a bit she added, "There's not a bit of telling what we will do, but I think we will at least act sanely. But we don't intend to step off now." On the thirteenth, just before she mailed the letter, she inserted a parenthesis after her statement about being sure of going to Peking. It read, "Later Oct. 13. not going now." There was no explanation even in the letter that she wrote to her mother on the night of the thirteenth. Not until her letter written on Oct. twenty third did it become clear what had transpired.

Reading between the lines, I believe that Hamp's letter written to her on October the tenth, which remarkably was postmarked as arriving in Shanghai on the twelfth, actually helped her to make up her mind not to go to Peking. In the letter he capitulates to the argument that Bibb's work is more definite than his. He still considers his calling to be a matter of conscience between himself and God, but this cannot be finalized until he knows her decision. She had asked some very probing questions about their relationship. He wrote, "Now let me see if I can answer your questions plainly. 'How essential is your coming or staying to my happiness?'(sic)" My father was not a person who revealed himself to others; and, yet he wrote,

> You are the only girl I ever <u>seriously</u> asked to marry me. I have been engaged once but in a very flippant sort of way. I have no other person in mind whom I care to ask to share my lot. It is not a matter of business that I think every single missionary should tend to. As to how much my happiness depends on it, I do not know. I try to

make it a business of my life to bow to the hand
of Providence and be contented and happy. One
thing I do feel sure of; God would not object to my
enjoying the pleasant memories of Hawkeye State.
If our lots are cast separately, it will be some time
before I marry, but I would not say that I would
never marry any one else. It might be that I would
not but I <u>hope</u> time and God would teach me to
love another. It would be <u>sad</u> if not."

He is still certain that Dr. Ray will tell them to go
Hwangshein. If, however, he were to tell them that
Shanghai was a more needy field, the only thing that
would keep him from coming would be his conscience
to God, and that was not yet fixed. She need not worry
about peer pressure. Not only was he sorry that he had
brought it up, but it would never be strong enough to
keep him from joining her. She should never question
his "manliness" to withstand peer pressure. Bibb had
asked him if he loved her as much as she loved him.
To which he replied that he had never seen anything to
compare with a women's love; it was a source of wonder
to him. Nevertheless, he did not want to get into the
business of comparing their love for each other. He was
sure of her love for him. He admitted to have never been
demonstrative, but he hoped that would change. "All I
can say is that I have tried to give you all there is to a
cold-hearted, matter-of-fact fellow. . ." She had also asked
him if he were to come to Shanghai, would it be because
of her ? And, wouldn't that be unbecoming? Hamp
answers: "It gives my heart great joy to know you think so
much of me, but there is Another (sic) to whom you owe
allegiance- and <u>first</u> and <u>greatest</u> love. I would not take

His place at all." If God wants you to stay in Shanghai, then you should stay and leave the rest to Him."

Hamp has already arranged living quarters for Bibb near the language school at the home of a missionary with the American Board. It was a large room and would have to be shared. Winnie Bennett would like to room with her if she agreed, but there was an immediate need to know what she planned to do, since someone else wanted the room. Would she please telegraph him at the language school what her decision would be? Would she please be frank and open about what she would like to do? If she wanted to wait for Dr. Ray's decision, that would be alright also. If she wanted some other living arrangement, that also could be made. He also agreed with a suggestion she had made in previous letter that they not plan to get married until the end of the first year in language school. This letter was signed, "As ever, Hamp"

Bibb's letter to her mother on October twenty third explains in detail what had happened since the fourteenth. She began the letter: "I've had the most unusual experiences I ever had during the past week and, if at any time in my long, long life I have needed you it is now and during this week." She continued,

> . . .a wee bit about events (ten pages). The last letter stated that I wasn't going to Peking. I came to that conclusion as the result of not hearing from Dr. Ray. Being providentially hindered from making the trip with either of two parties going there that week (sic). and a strange and sudden change in my feeling that I should not go although for two or three days I had had my plans made to go if Hamp

> wanted me, i.e. if he answered some questions I'd asked satisfactorily – he did, but I wired him to let the room he had engaged for me go and before my message was received he wired, 'Coming for you, leaving Saturday.'

The telegram arrived while Bibb was studying and Miss Kelly received it. Miss Kelly seemed as excited and pleased as Bibb. The word got around the mission rather rapidly and Sunday afternoon they called a station meeting at the home of Mr. and Mrs. Roger Steel in order to give a cordial welcome to Mr. Ware and invite him to remain in Shanghai. He was to be recruited for the North Gate Church work and would be given the oversight of the gym there and the evangelistic work of the church which included eight outstations. The single women, Misses Kelly, Priest, Johnson, Marlow, Lynn, Garrett and Bibb had supper together and then joined most of the rest of the mission to meet Hamp at the railroad station at ten o'clock in the evening. Only Mr. Steel and Bibb were allowed to go on to the railroad platform to meet him, but as he came through the gate, they all sang, "How do you do Mr. Ware, how do you do? Is there anything that we can do for you? We will do the best we can, standing by you like a man. How do you do Mr. Ware, how do you do?" After they came home Miss Kelly allowed them to stay up until twelve o'clock by which time they had decided on a course of action. Whether Hamp stayed or went back north, they would act together. In other words, whatever Hamp did, Mary Bibb would do also.

The nest morning a friend from the Y.M.C.A. went over a map of Shanghai with Hamp to show him the opportunities that the city offered. The Steels had invited them to dinner with a number of other guests including Dr. and Mrs. Chambers from Canton, Mr. and Mrs. Mc Neil Poteat from Kaifung, Dr. and Mrs. Mac Millan from Soochow, and the Rogers who were members of the Shanghai station. That afternoon Hamp made his decision to stay in Shanghai. Bibb wrote, ". . .we believe it was direct answer to prayer. All of us had tried to know God's will and follow it unselfishly and gladly and it was good when he decided we would stay." With out so much as a paragraph break in the letter her next sentence launched into their plans, "The next thing to plan was the wedding – Miss Priest said I must have a veil and would not listen to my wearing my pretty plum purple suit even and after we set last Tuesday for a simple wedding with just the family we changed the date until Oct. 25(sic)." You can read the excitement in the letter by the way it was written. Often words and punctuations were omitted. Bibb wrote out in hand an invitation to her parents:

Judge and Mrs. C.P. Long of Tupelo, Miss.
Request the honor of your presence
At the marriage of their daughter
Mary Bibb
to
Mr. James Hamilton Ware
of Atlanta, Ga.
At the home of Miss Willie Kelly
466 Rue La Fayette
Shanghai, China
Oct. 25, 1921
At 5:00 P.M.

The next few days Bibb spent in making her wedding dress. She and Miss Kelly went to a Chinese fabric shop and bought some very light cream colored silk-satin-like material. Originally she had thought that she would make the dress out of white organdy; but when ever she thought about it, she would remember her mother's stories about the Piney Woods wedding and the bride's dotted Swiss dress. Bibb immediately began to work on the dress, but when it became apparent that she might not finish it in time, her friend Mrs. Bills had her tailor help finish it for her. The dress was of a unique two-piece design. The first piece was a sleeveless full-length dress with puffs at the hips where the skirt began. The second part was a long sleeved, waist length apron like vest that slipped over the head and was tied with two attached sashes into a falling bow behind her back. It was very smart looking and set her figure off quite well. The most intricate parts of the dress, which took her an immense time to make, were numerous very small beaded ornaments. These were made with a two-inch circle of very fine beads that surrounded several dangling two inched loops of the same beads. They were scattered over the dress as though they were part of the material itself. The dress was quite stunning. Mother wore the dress to dinner each anniversary thereafter. She wore it well into the nineteen forties when it was necessary to wear a sturdy corset to get into it. It is still a part of the family archives as is part of the corsage that Edith Whisenhunt made for her to carry during the wedding.

In her letter she raved about how good and sweet Miss Kelly, Miss Priest, Eph and Edith Whisenhunt, and Mrs. Bills had been. It was not like having the wedding at home, and she missed not having her mother there. If their furlough had not been so far away she would have like the wedding to be in Tupelo. However, ". . .the family here are doing all they can for our happiness – I've never seen such tireless effort on behalf of friends of so short an acquaintance.(sic)" One evening Miss Priest had said, "Mary Bibb it won't be like it would be at home, but there's lots of love in it." Her friends had called the guest on the telephone, helped select the pattern for her dress, helped to cut it out and fitted it, and they had planned the program for the day. She intended to place her family's picture on the mantel in the living room and her friends from the U.S. in frames hidden among the shrubs and flowers that festooned the living room. The decorations would include ferns, palms, dahlias, and pink and white carnations. While Eph Whisenhunt preformed the ceremony, Bibb said that she planned to be looking at the picture of her parents. Miss Kelly and Miss Priest had even planned the reception that was to follow the wedding. They would serve chicken salad, cheese straws, sandwiches, coffee or tea, and cake. Miss Kelly playfully called some of the chickens that wondered around the compound feeding, "wedding chickens."

After telling her mother of her wedding plans, Bibb became quite effusive about Hamp. "Miss Priest thinks he is perfection, said she would rather have him than waffles." Eph and Edith Whisenhunt thought of him as a brother. ". . . for my part I don't like him – he is my sweetheart – I can't say anything nice about him because he is going to read this, but I think he is a m-a-n, that any girl might be proud to call her husband. . . . Some things about our association together and courtship are too sacred to me to write where I don't know who might read this but some day I'll tell you all I've wanted to this week." Bibb winds up her adulations by saying that he is very smart and will learn Chinese much more rapidly than she will. He plays the trumpet and is handy with almost everything. Having been in the navy he can wash and iron is own clothes. "He is alright, and I know we will have a happy home." But, it will be a year or two before they leave Miss Kelly's at Rue Lafayette.

On the day before the wedding they received a letter from Dr. Ray telling Bibb to go to Hwangshien. However, Dr. Ray had ambiguously sent Hamp's baggage on to Shanghai. Consequently, at everyone's suggestion, they were going to ignore the instructions for the time being.

On the morning of their wedding day, October twenty fifth, Bibb added this postscript to the letter begun on the twenty third, "My wedding day and one made to order – beautiful – will write again soon & in detail. Wish you were all here. Bushels of love from Bibb and Hamp (sic)."

The boat carrying mail back to the U.S. did not sail until November the second. Consequently the family in Tupelo received on the same day the letter begun on October twenty third written before the wedding and the letter begun on October thirty first telling the details of the wedding itself.

On the morning of the wedding day Hamp helped with the decorations and Bibb worked on her dress. Bibb said that when she came down for the noon meal," I was tired then and didn't feel very 'bride-fied' – even forgot I didn't have on a petticoat, but had on a dark skirt (sic)."

Around three o'clock she began dressing; and, as she put it, ". . .like a wise virgin by four thirty I was awaiting the groom with nose, not lamp, brightly shining and face burning." Hannah Plowden, a friend from the Women's Missionary Union Training School, and Miss Kelly helped her dress and kept her company. Sharply at five she heard the music "Souvenir" begin and then the Bridle Chorus from Lohengren. Miss Kelly gave her a kiss for Mer as she started. "In spite of a perfectly composed mind I found it hard to keep from wobbling and trembling until I reached Hamp who was awaiting me at the foot of the stairs-pacing to and fro as a spirited young horse." The ceremony was very tradition; it could have come out of almost any Protestant service manual. Eph, as the minister, carried out his part well. The pastor of Old North Gate Church, Pastor Sung, gave the benediction in Chinese, which neither of them understood, but could only sense by the tone of his voice that it was a long and ardent blessing. Following the ceremony Miss Kelly stepped forward to direct people to the reception and was the first to call Bibb, Mrs. Ware. During the reception and following it a photographer took pictures, copies of which Bibb promised to send home to the family. Several days later she took her bouquet that Edith Whisenhunt had made for her, dipped it in paraffin to preserve it, and sent part of it to her mother.

The Wares had been invited to go to Chinkiang for their honeymoon, but decided against it. Language study was too important to spend so much time away. In stead they spent their wedding night at the Palace Hotel which was, at the time, the most stylish hotel in Shanghai. For years the myth was whispered around by their children that they had stayed at Rue Lafayette and that Miss Kelly had not let them shut the door to their room that night. No one checked the accuracy of the myth with the principles.

The origin of the myth lies somewhere in the imaginations of members of the family. It probably was started as a, not too kind, tongue in cheek commentary on Miss Kelly, whom we all thought had opposed the wedding until we discovered mother's letters.

On the twenty-sixth Hamp and Bibb left the hotel in the afternoon to do some sightseeing. Everything in Shanghai apart from the mission was new to them. They began with the Royal Asiatic Museum and the Shanghai Library, and then moved on into the old walled city to the Temple of the Queen of Heaven. After spending a pleasant afternoon and evening wandering around from place to place, the Chocolate Shop was their last stop. Here Hamp bought his new bride a box of chocolates. When they returned home they were welcomed warmly and their room had been prepared, in Bibb's words, "perfectly," for them. For the next few days the newly weds were dinned and entertained by friends. The Steels, who were the senior missionaries in the mission, had them to dinner, and Hannah Plowden, Bibb's friend from Training School, invited them together with the Whisenhunts to the University for an afternoon visit and dinner. However, by the end of the week it was back to work five hours a day on language study and orientation. On Sunday they had their introduction to the Shanghai missionaries' association, and were asked to stand in the receiving line to meet the people from other Protestant denomination who were serving in the city. In the evenings during the week both of them had begun to read Giles' <u>China and The Chinese</u> as part of their introduction to Chinese history and culture. Both of them were slowly settling down from the excitement and beginning to find their place in the Shanghai mission. The letter that Bibb had begun to her mother on Halloween ended on November First. She wrote, "Last night was the calmest Halloween I ever spent." She missed being at home and being a part of Olivia's Halloween party.

By November the sixth, when the next letter was begun, the weather had turned cold.

[i] Immanuel C.Y. Hsu, <u>The Rise of Modern China</u>, Oxford, 1970, p. 561.

CHAPTER FOUR

Rue Lafayette

When Bibb had finished reading Giles' <u>China and the Chinese</u>, she wrote to her mother that the book ". . . had upset some of our old time ideas of China and her people – it is very interesting though out of date in many details as regards life in Shanghai." Hamp and Mary Bibb lived their first few years in Shanghai with Miss Kelly and Miss Priest at 466 Rue Lafayette. It was here that they began their Chinese language studies along with the Whisenhunts, and it was from here that they began their work as missionaries at Old Northgate Church. The Rue Lafayette compound was in the French Concession, the center of foreign residential affluence. Old North Gate Church, on the other hand, was at the North Gate to the old Chinese walled city, and consequently on the very edge of the cities worst slums.

In the 1920s Shanghai was unquestionably the most modern city in Asia, but it was also a city of extremes. Chinese and foreign interests clashed. It was one of the most colonial cities in the world, although it was not a colony of any one country; and it was also one of the most nationalistic centers of Chinese aspirations. Extreme wealth and poverty existed side by side, as did missionary puritan ethics and the free-for-all vices of the nightclubs and brothels which were almost everywhere in the city.

Geographically, the city was divided into four major territorial divisions: the old walled Chinese city, the French Concession, the International Concession, and Chapei. Other areas on the outskirts of the concessions were known as Greater Shanghai. Where you lived in the city, what your nationality happened to be, and your vocation determine to a large degree the life you lived. Businessmen and missionaries for the most part lived their respective lives quite separately. There was not much social interaction between them. Occasionally, national communities would meet for a celebration of their heritage, such as the Fourth of July; but the encounters were often more patriotic than they were personal interaction between social groups.

The foremost feature of the city and its driving dynamic was unregulated capitalism. If you were an entrepreneur, Shanghai offered unlimited opportunities. With adequate initial capital almost any business was destined to succeed. The one constant that could be counted on was the growth of businesses, banking, and industries. Shanghai was the center of Chinese modernization and industrial growth. As it grew, it became the center of commercial life for all of East Asia.

Until the nineteenth century Shanghai was unremarkable. Around 200 B.C. the little village where fishermen traded was known as Hu-tuh. It began to be called Shanghai (Above the Sea) in about 1280, but it was still not much more than a small fishing and trading village. Japanese pirates sometimes raided the village and a wall four to five miles long and twenty-three feet high with six gates and twenty arrow towers was built around it in 1554. It had almost no significance in earlier Chinese history. However, its location up the Hwanpoo River just a few miles from the mouth of the Yangtze River gave it a tremendous advantage over other coastal ports in the late Ching Dynasty. The Yangtze River was the central trade route to over half of Interior China, and the deep water anchorages along the Hwangpoo were sheltered from the flow of the big river and from the Yellow Sea and Pacific Ocean. Foreign traders saw it for its potential.

The first foreigner settlers to come to Shanghai were the British who arrived there shortly after the Treaty of Nanking (1842). Hugh Hamilton Lindsay, an employee of the East India Company, had visited Shanghai in 1832 and recognized it value as a trade center. The Treaty of Nanking, which followed the Opium War, gave to the British the right to establish five trading ports along China's Maritime Provinces. Shanghai was one of these ports. The British opened a consulate in Shanghai in 1843, and wasted no time in setting themselves up. A year later the Americans and the French signed treaties with China that gave them the same rights as the British. It was not long before the Americans and French also developed their own settlements or concessions.

Under the Treaty of Nanking and subsequent treaties, forced on the Chinese by other countries, many foreigners were not accountable to Chinese magistrates or Chinese laws. These extraterritorial privileges were eventually extended to the citizens of fourteen nation under "favored nations" treaties: The United States, Britain, France, Belgium, Brazil, Denmark, Italy, Japan, The Netherlands, Norway, Spain, Portugal, Sweden, and Switzerland each had their place. Nationals from these countries were tried or sued in their own national courts and not in Chinese courts. Violators of law and legal cases involving foreign nationals were handled in the consular courts, by special judges appointed by the governments of the foreign residence, or by the governing body of a given concession. Those foreigners not included in the "favored nations" treaties such as Russians and Germans (after World War I) were subject to Chinese courts. Foreign military were not subject to the Consular Courts or the Municipal court, but to the military police and military authority of their respective nationalities. One of the most extraordinary events that developed was the placing of the Chinese Customs Service under foreign control. Foreigners collected duties and regulated immigration. Even after World War II when formal control of the Customs Service was turned over to the Chinese, British citizens ran the Chinese Customs Service in Shanghai. I had a run in with a wiry redheaded Englishman of the Chinese Customs Service when we returned to Shanghai in 1946. He insisted that the little pump action 22-caliber sporting gun that I brought with me was not a gun at all, but a rifle. It took me several months to get it cleared through customs.

The first American settlement was not a trading post but an enclave north of Soochow Creek in the Hongkew District. Bishop William J. Boone of the American Episcopal Church Mission established it in 1848. An American consulate was not posted until 1854. Finding it to their mutual advantage the British and American Concessions were merged in 1863 to form the International Concession. The French and International Concessions began with relatively small areas of land, approximately three hundred acres; but grew over time to cover over seven thousand acres. In spite of there being extraterritorial rights by the foreigners living in these areas, the land was still considered to be under the sovereignty of the Chinese government.

Shanghai was a vulnerable city. A secret, anti-imperial society called the "Small Swords" actually took over the Chinese walled city from the Imperial forces in 1853 and held it for two years. It became obvious that the foreign settlements needed to organize their own defenses. The Volunteer Corp was formed, and fought its first engagement against the Ching Dynasty forces at The Battle of Muddy Flat (1854), in what is today the People's Park in the center of downtown. Seeing the need for closer cooperation, the foreign residence set up the Municipal Council to coordinate their interests. By the end of the century the Council had established a Fire Department, secured the water supply, and bought the Electrical Light Company. A Ratepayers Association was formed to determine taxes for the running of the city and determine who would serve on the Municipal Council. It would be a number of years before Chinese served in the Volunteer Corp, and not until 1920 that they served in an advisory capacity to the Municipal Council and formed their own Ratepayers Association.

The volunteers were never solely on their own. As long as I can remember there was always a combination of foreign naval vessels anchored in the Whangpoo to protect foreign interests. As a child growing up I can remember a British and/or American cruiser and several destroyers in a line, swinging on anchor with the tide just off the Bund, Shanghai's waterfront main street. American, British, French, Japanese, Italians and other nations routinely deployed gunboats up the Yangtze to guarantee the protection of foreign interests. This lasted up to the Second World War.

A greater challenge came with the Taiping Rebellion, a religious and political revolt against the Imperial rule. Hung Hsui-chuan, the founder and leader of the Taiping, was a young unsuccessful Chinese scholar from near Canton. Hung was a village teacher and an avid reader. Having failed his government sponsored Confucian scholar's exams several times, he turned to reading Christian tracts given to him by a missionary, Edwin Stevens. During a particularly difficult time in his life following his third failure at the exams, Hung underwent a revolutionary conversion. He began to see himself as a Messianic figure. At one point Hung attempted to convert to Christianity and began studying with a Southern Baptist Missionary, Issachar J. Roberts. Unfortunately, Roberts' other students became jealous and told Hung he would should ask for a payment for being baptized. Unaware of his students' treachery toward Hung, Roberts rebuffed him. Hung and his cousin proceeded to baptize one another. Soon Hung began referring to himself as the Heavenly King and began to set up a Heavenly Kingdom in which the Chinese were God's chosen people who would bring in the Great Peace (Taiping). The movement had a special appeal to the poor because it advocated the sharing of means. Hung and his followers tried to establish land redistribution for each family, the equality of women, the unification of military and civilian rule, and the unity of culture and religion. The Ten Commandments became fundamental and social welfare programs were put in place. By 1849 Hung had recruited thousands to the new religion and its revolution. After marching north to the Yangtze he set up his kingdom in Nanking around 1850. The Taiping was in a real sense the first indigenous Christian movement in China, but it had the misfortune of disrupting trade and the existing law and order of the Ching Dynasty.

At first foreigners were neutral to the movements partly because they knew very little about it. At the height of the Taiping Movement, when it covered almost a third of East China, it began to fall apart internally because of rivalries between the leaders. As some of the heterodox teachings of the group became know, missionaries, in particular, began to turn their backs on the movement. For foreigners the final straw was the movement of the Taiping on Shanghai and other trade cities from 1860-1864. In 1860 the Shanghai settlements rose up against the movement. Under the leadership of Frederick Townsend Ward, who became a Chinese citizen in order to lead the Imperial troops, they engaged the Taiping. When Ward was killed in battle near Ningpo, an illustrious Brit, Charles George Gordon, followed his leadership. Gordon would go on to defeat the Taiping in 1864 and then make a name for himself in British history when he was killed as the defender of Khartoum in North Africa several years later.

For the most part Shanghai was relatively free of large military conflicts, even though there was a war between Great Britain and France and the Chinese in 1856-60, and between France and China over what is now Vietnam in 1881-85. Anti-missionary movements in 1891 and the Sino-Japanese War of 1894 had little or no affect on the city. Occasionally there were riots when the Municipal Counsel raised taxes or there were demonstrations against the Japanese. Even the Boxer Rebellion in 1900 failed to cause problems in Shanghai. The only sizable disturbance happened in 1905 when the jurisdiction of the Mixed Court was called into question. A landing party of foreign troops was required to put down the demonstration. No major problems arose during the 1911 Revolution, and it was not until 1913 when a second revolution against Yuan Shihkai took place that there was any real fighting around the city. Although this took place in the Chinese parts of the city, it never the less drew foreign troop intervention.

One of the consequences of World War I was the return of many foreign nationals to their nations of origin. This was not a major setback for the city, but it did slow down its expansion. It created a problem particularly for German nationals. A more profound impact on the city came as White Russians, fleeing the Bolshevik Revolution, began to filter into the city. Most of them had lost everything. Some had actually walked across Siberia to escape. Other had defected from the Russian Navy. Some had come down from Vladivostok through Harbin and Manchuria. All of them seemed to have been dirt poor. When they arrived in Shanghai, there were no jobs, and many of them wound up doing coolly labor. It was not uncommon in the wintertime for them to die on the streets and doorways of businesses where they had sought shelter. The women survived better than the men by turning to prostitution. They became the leading "madams" of the dance halls, bars and brothels.

Winter in Shanghai was often cold and damp. The cold Siberian winds whipped down from the north across the flat deltas of the east coast with nothing to stop them. Puddles and small ponds often had thin layers of ice, but Shanghai seldom had snow. If it did fall, it was no more than two or three inches and would melt in a day or two. The moisture from the sea mixed with the freezing air made it deadly for those who had to live on the streets without housing. The average Chinese home was seldom heated. Some times there were small charcoal burners that were used for cooking that were a source of warmth. But most Chinese simply put on an extra layer or two of clothing. Men and women still wore either long robes as outerwear or Chinese pants and jackets that were padded with either cotton or raw silk. Of course the raw silk ones were much more expensive, but they were lighter and warmer. Chinese workers' footwear was less satisfactory. Shoes were not made of leather but of cloth and had more or less water resistant soles. Both Chinese and foreigners slept under cotton, down, or silk stuffed blankets in their homes. There was very little heating even in businesses. Some of the wealthy Chinese and foreigners had coal fired steam radiator heat in their homes. Many of the homes simply had coal burning fireplaces or cast iron stoves. Gas heat and cooking came to Shanghai early in the twentieth century, but the pipelines were primarily in the French and International Settlements. Shanghai had electricity from the late nineteenth century, but it was far too expensive to use for heating. The occasional electric heater, which was used only in emergencies and in very small spaces, was made with either a radiant electric coil, or in some cases a small electric fan to disperse the heat. Kerosene heaters came later. The imported kerosene ones burned with large

but even more pleased that he was going back to Old Miss. She hoped that he would be a strong Christian gentleman there. She wrote about Gen's (her sister-in-law) and Snooks' (Gen's daughter) trip to Little Rock. She talked about their neighbors, Mrs. Pegues, Mrs. Berry, and Mrs. Black, and said: "I'd like to fly back and be present at one of those back-door gatherings." She wondered whether Julia, her sister, had found a place to live in Atlanta, and how Papa was doing and if he had a happy birthday. Was he more reconciled to her leaving? She confesses that she thought about him in her quiet hours. There had been a fire at Aunt Estelle's house, and she hoped it was not too bad. In her letter she sent congratulations to Mr. and Mrs. Chisholm, but its not clear why. The list of Tupelo people goes on. She would have liked to see Mrs. Willis, and she is sorry that Mrs. Reed, Mrs. Clark, and Dr. Garmon are leaving town. "People seem to so much nearer when they are in Tupelo than any where else." She said Hamp is still wonderful, so kind and thoughtful. She wrote that the Wares and the Wisenhunts have two Chinese teachers, Mr. Sung and Mr. Si, and are studying hard. "If we could just talk and be busy at the things we long to do we'd have no time [to] be homesick and lonely. It is when we aren't busy and have time to think that we get in the 'dumps'. I'd give just about all I have to spend this afternoon with you. Mother dear." She closes the letter with: "Give Gran, Aunt Laura, Estelle, all the uncles and cousins, friends, neighbors, and loved ones heaps of love, among them Olivia, Layette, Coz Fan, Edmunds, Mrs. Ford, Aunt Fannie, the Wilsons, Katsi, Mrs. Insure, and 'my children' at church." Homesickness was just a thought away.

In her letter on Armistice Day, November Eleventh, she wrote: "I've my telescope on Tupelo now and I am looking right into 543 Jefferson St. to see what you are doing. Oh! I see you and you are all peacefully sleeping, but it is 'most time to rise and then I can hear 'Pop' in the kitchen putting the bacon in the stove, Miss Liv is sleepily making up beds, Grand reading the Bible, and you, Mer, are here, there, and everywhere busy with the day's tasks."

The days at Rue Lafayette were getting more routine. They began with a family, morning devotional around seven, breakfast and then language study with their Chinese teachers from nine until lunchtime. In the afternoon there was often a class to supervise at Old North Gate Church or time to take shopping trip or outing before dinnertime. After dinner it was back to language study and devotionals at bedtime. My father, who seems to have been much more at ease with the Chinese students he taught, adapted to spoken Chinese much more rapidly than the others. Mother and the Wisenhunts seemed to have difficulty with the seven different tones used to distinguish meaning in Shanghai dialect. Reading Chinese characters was difficult, but it was not nearly as difficult as speaking or writing. Mother never really learned to speak Chinese without a pronounced foreign accent, where as my Father became so fluent that it was impossible, even for Chinese, to tell that he was not a native speaker. Mother told a story on herself; one of her teacher Mr. Si was drilling the group when Mother made a remark in response to Mr. Si's statement that his cloths were warm because they were padded. Her response in Chinese was "Ngou kuk izang z lang sz." which translated meant, "My cloths are cold water." Needless to say Mr. Si, Hamp, the Wisenhunts, were very amuse.

When she tried to mend matters, she said, her cloths were "kai", a terms used for hot water. The group spend about five hours a day in language study.

Both my Father and Mother learned to read Chinese well, but I have not found any documents in which either of them wrote in Chinese characters. Their writing seems to have been limited to short notes, or instructions written on a blackboard while they were teaching.

Language study was more than the study of the Chinese language. It was a two-year course that had been designed by the Soochow mission for their new missionaries. Not only was it structured to make one fluent in Chinese language, but also to be conversant in Chinese history and culture. Students met with their Chinese teachers for several hours each weekday primarily to learn the language. Even though some of the teachers were not Christians, the basic written text that was studied was the Bible. First year students learn to read the first ten chapters of the Gospel of John. In addition they were to learn to recognize 400 characters, plus be able to write an essay using at least 200 characters. Each student was to commit to memory a minimum of ten colloquial expressions, ten Chinese proverbs, the Lord's Prayer, and ten verses of Scripture. Beyond their language studies they were to learn the names of the different Chinese provinces and their capitals and become familiar with Chinese geography in general. English reading included: Dawson's, Ethics of Confucius; Hackman's, Buddhism as a Religion; a translation of the Tao Te Ching; Giles', Chinese Literature; Werner's, China and the Chinese; and E. C. Moore's, West and East. In addition to these assignments each new missionary had some responsibility in a church or a school that immersed him or her both in the language and in social interaction.

The second year of language studies included intense conversational Chinese and the reading of Luke-Acts. 400 more characters were to be learned and an essay was to be written using 500 characters, 80% of which were to be in the student's own calligraphy. In the other 20%, where it was necessary, a student could use terms that were Romanized or phonetically spelled. As part of their learning experience, each student was to give a fifteen-minute address to a Chinese audience or conduct a Bible Class in Chinese. The second year reading included: Bunyan's, Pilgrim's Progress (Part I); F.W. Baller's edition of Sacred Edicts; F. D. Hawk Pott's, <u>A Sketch of Chinese History</u>; Kenneth Scott Latourette's, <u>The Development of China</u>; Martin's, <u>The Lore of Cathay</u>; Weiger's. <u>Chinese Tenets and Customs</u>; and Henk's, <u>The Philosophy of Wang Yang Ming.</u> "In retrospect it seems surprising that none of Sun Yat Sen's writings, or writings about him and the republican movement, were required reading. Possibly, it was because Sun and the republican movement were too contemporary and their thoughts were consequently constantly changing.

As language studies intensified in November, so did the need to shop for Christmas gifts for the folks back home. Letters to and from the United States usually took about three to four weeks each way. Packages took from a month to six weeks to cross the Pacific.

One of the better places to buy gifts to be sent home was an area around the Roman Catholic Cathedral in Zi Ka Wei, which was just south and east of the French Concession. Chinese Roman Catholics made up the majority of the population in Zi Ka Wei. They numbered several thousands and many of them were quite wealth. Their schools were run by Jesuit priests, and their communal daycare nurseries for their working constituents were excellent. The Cathedral sponsored many of the small home industries like furniture making and the manufacturing of brass goods such as fire-place sets, bells, trays, kettles, and Chinese hot water bottles (a round, water tight brass containers that was put between the sheets before you went to bed, and which you were very careful not to touch because you could easily get burned). The area was also known for its woodcarving, embroidery, and laces. One afternoon the Wares and Wisenhunts went to Zi Ka Wei to sightsee and shop for Christmas gifts.

By the middle of November Hamp and Mary Bibb had been introduced to the entire missionary community. They were asked to stand in the receiving line at the Missionary Association meeting that met every first Tuesday of each month for lunch and discussion of current topics of interest. Both of them were becoming more involved in the life of Old North Gate Church and school. Some of the boys were coming over one evening for a social gathering and to play American games. Bibb also wrote that she was looking forward to an evangelistic meeting at the church. She was concerned for some of the girls that she was helping to teach because they had not yet responded to the Christian message.

Hamp's trunk arrived from Peking about the middle of the month. Two of his heavy suits of underwear, his raincoat, a pair of gym shoes, two gold stick pens and several Mexican dollars had been taken out his trunk. He hoped to be reimbursed by American Express since they were responsible for sending his belongings from Peking to Shanghai. Bibb was looking forward to packages coming to them for Christmas and instructed her mother to send anything under fifty pounds through the postal system. Anything larger should be shipped directly to China to the offices of the Associated Mission Treasurer and the original bill of laden sent by mail directly to her.

Even though Thanksgiving dinner was to be spent with the Rogers and the Steels, Bibb confesses,

> "We will think of you, however, and be thankful you are ours to love, write to, think of and pray for. I can't be thankful enough for the blessings God has given me in letting me come to my 'Dream-land,' giving me a happy home with congenial friends, the best of men for my husband, health and strength and a vision of home in my dreams and imagination. Imagination is a wonderful gift, for I can see you often in my minds eye when the waves of the ocean and the mountain and plains and valleys cut off the view."

Even though it was not yet thanksgiving Bibb could not get her mind off what Christmas would be like in Tupelo while she was writing. She would give anything to see Little Gen on Christmas day. Would she be hanging her stocking up there at 543 Jefferson? How was "Gran," her Grandmother? Wasn't it a coincidence that she and her sister Julia both married men from Atlanta, Georgia, who both went to the University of Georgia?

Bibb sent home a picture of the inaugural meeting of a choir at Old North Gate Church and identified for her family all of her friends. All of the choir members were so well educated; many of them had attended the Baptist College in Shanghai. One of the first things that the choir was thinking of doing was to carol the invalids in Old North Gate Church. Some of the older women in the picture were white haired, and she remarked that so many of them wore a braided coil of coal black hair on the back of their heads. From the time I was a child I do not remember my mother with any other kind of hairdo. She always wore her hair twisted and in a bun on the back of her head whether it was dark or white.

The first indication that everything was not going well with their closest friends the Wisenhunts came in the same letter. Edith was not feeling well. She was being bothered by her nerves and she had a very bad cold. The rest of the household on Rue Lafayette were doing well. Miss Sallie Priest wrote Bibb's mother to thank her for Bibb and Hamp. She reassures her about Hamp with a Chinese saying that she roughly translated, "Let your heart be at rest on that subject." The bond between Miss Priest and my mother was growing stronger and stronger. When summer came, Bibb would be taking over Miss Priest work while she went back to the U.S. on furlough.

Bibb's letters get longer in November, and there are more references to home in Tupelo. She asks again whether Papa was more reconciled to her being away, and how was his health. She hoped he had a happy birthday, and added, "We remember him in our quiet hour."

Their days at Rue Lafayette began with reading three chapters from the Old Testament alone, and one from the New Testament at family worship, plus selections and comments in her daily meditation book. She and Hamp planned to read through the entire Bible together. Hamp she said, ". . . is too good to live, intensely practical –wouldn't (sic) not care if he were a bit more frivolous and less dignified, and just as tender and sweet as can be." She said she never did like for people to talk about her affairs, but supposed some would be saying, "I thought so. Can it be possible? A good old maid spoiled. Who is he? How does he look? etc."

Her mind floats between Tupelo and Shanghai. At one moment she is telling Mer that she hopes Aunt Estelle's house in Tupelo was not to badly damaged by fire and that Mer had attended the Tupelo Saturday P.M. Reading Club and enjoyed it very much. She sent congratulations to Mr. and Mrs. Chisholm, and wished that she had seen Mrs. Willis when she was there. Mrs. Willis had sent a beautiful pair of black hose. She is so sorry that Mrs. Reed, Mrs. Clark, and Mrs. Gardner are leaving. "People seem so much nearer when they are in Tupelo than anywhere else." Shellie had not written since they parted in Yokahama, and she doesn't know her address. Montgomery Ward had not gotten her things to her, but she expected them soon.

With all of the excitement of the wedding and getting settled in, there had been no time for home sickness. But it begins to appear in Bibb's November ninth letter.

"If we could just talk and be busy at the things we long to do we'd have no time be (sic) homesick and lonely, It is when we aren't busy to have time to think that we get in the 'dumps'. I'd give just about all that I have to spend this afternoon with you, Mother, dear. But I must not dwell on my desire to be there for I want you to be happy and feel glad I'm here. I am alright and I think you need never worry about me, only pray I may be strong and brave to do His will and abide in Him always."

She closes the letter by remembering Mer's Sunday School promotion exercises and instructing her mother to give her love to all the family and friends in Tupelo. "Love galore to every one. Bibb."

The November eleventh letter starts out nostalgically. Bibb has her imaginary telescope focused on 543 Jefferson Street., but the letter soon turns to the events of her day. As usual the day began with breakfast, devotionals and language study. Rose Marlowe and Mary Nell Lynn, who worked with the Cantonese church, were there for lunch, and all the ladies packed themselves in the car and went shopping at Sie ka wei, the predominantly Roman Catholic community in Shanghai. The area was named for a Chinese minister in the Ching government who had converted to Catholicism. Among the Chinese sections of Shanghai. it was one of the most prosperous and attractive. The cathedral was beautiful and the shops and homes in the area were exceptionally well kept. They were amazed at the quality and variety of things to buy there.

The letters from the latter part of November tell of a full social life. Dr. Ray, his wife, and secretary will be coming in December. Several families have come through Shanghai on their way to the interior and North China. The W.W, Stouts and their four children came through on their way to Hwanghien. Miss Lynn was leaving for the U.S. Everyone is looking forward to Christmas. The issue of homesickness seems to be on everyone's mind. Bibb is quite blunt about the reasons for homesickness that were in her mother's last letter. "I do not like one bit though the part of your letter that assigns reasons for not being homesick- the reasons do not stand to reason and are false." The letter does not tell us what those reasons were. It is becoming more apparent that Edith Wisenhunt is getting particularly home sick. Bibb says, "Edith is so homesick every time she gets a letter she can't enjoy it.- I think I love you as much as she loves home but I either control myself by casting off desires that can't possibly be gratified before they take root good or take out the feeling by a chat with you. Edith will make herself sick if she doesn't quit giving way, for she is so nervous and not a bit strong."

Christmas presents have already been sent; a pongee for Mer, pearls for Olivia, some extra ordinarily good tea for Papa, and a luncheon set for Julia. Snooks was to get a little pongee dress in a butterfly pattern that Bibb knew would please Gen and Sam. Bibb included some additional pictures of Hamp and Miss Priest, the grave of Mathew T. Yates and his wife, along with presence of incense sticks for the Mer's Sunday School children.

Bibb did not mind sharing her family letters with their friends in Tupelo. She said, "If my letters can give any one any pleasure of course I' glad for them to be read, but not published. . ." She is never proud of the finished product because she had done a dozen other things while writing the letters. When she wrote personal letters she always made it plain to who she was writing, especially to Mer.

The letter closes by telling the family that they are going to hang up stockings and play Santa Clause to one another. Dr. Ray will be there and the whole mission will likely have lunch together. Her next letter to Mer will be private. The letter ends on an after thought of how good it would have been if she could have participated in the domino party at home; she thinks about how it would be to place each table and how jolly Papa would be.

No mention is made in the November and early December letters of Thanksgiving. Christmas is already on everyone's mind. Bibb says that she is not very excited about Christmas and has had dreams of being at home putting up curtains on bamboo poles. The drapes did not fit right and she remembered dreaming that she would be home next summer or on her furlough and could put them up right. She awoke with a sigh and Hamp asked her what was wrong. She told him, and he was all sympathy. Christmas was just not the same in Shanghai as it was in Tupelo.

Events changed fast at Rue Lafayette. As Bibb said, in one letter I'm telling you about bundling for the first time on foreign soil and in the next letter I'm telling you that I will have an appendicitis surgery. She reassured the folks at home that it will not be bad. She had had an acute attack the previous Monday, but Dr. Hiltner, who would perform the surgery, said that it was just a matter of time before she has another one. She is aware of the problem much of the time and thinks that it is a good thing to go ahead and get it over. She jokes that she will not have any more troubled with her digestion, "her feet will get warm; my cocked eye will straighten out; and all her freckles will disappear". The surgery would take place at Dr. Febring's hospital just around the corner. Dr. Hitlner, who is a Harvard graduate, has already taken out the appendix of several Baptist missionaries. She says she is not worried, but if anything were to go wrong that Hamp would cable them immediately. If, she were to die, it would be God's will and she would be with Jesus on His birthday. The surgery coming when it did of course meant that she would be in bed for Christmas and would not be able to "frolic about." Unfortunately the bed she will be stuck in is a bit smelly and will have to be aired several days. Hamps' bed is made of Japanese floss, but is in the wrong place to be use. They had been using their rooms to teach about fifty Chinese children. The children learn fast; they sang, "Away in Manger" that morning.

Each day brings her new insight into Chinese life. She and Miss Priest walked over to the Ningpo Guild house where they keep the bodies of the deceased until their families can save up enough money to buy a burial plot. Some times they have to be kept for years. About a half block behind their house there are numerous grave mounds and a road is being built through the area. The bones from the grave mounds are put into urns and reburied. There were a number of snakes that were living among the bones and urns which she thought must certainly have fed off the bodies. She discovered that the Chinese had a very different attitude toward the snakes. They were a welcomed presence.

According to the medical practice of the day, Bibb was in bed for two or more weeks; she seemed to have had some difficulty the first few days. Both the Chinese help and Hamilton brought her breakfast in bed. Hamp takes her up and down stairs in his arms, her private sedan chair, so that she doesn't really miss most of what is going on. Bibb refers to it like she did their courtship, and hopes that the end of their lives will be as good as it is right now. Hamp bought her a big arrangement of camellias. He knew Bibb's love of chocolates and brought her some before Christmas, and to top everything off had her wedding ring reset with platinum prongs. He said the candy was a hospital gift, the prongs were for Christmas.

Tupelo is always full of gossip and the news was planted around that Bibb and Hamp had planned their wedding months before. An angry Bibb made it clear that the two of them were not sure until the last minuet that they would be married as soon as they were. She claims that she fell in love with him when he wrapped her feet while they were out on the ship's deck and she was too sick to do it herself. Even the moon didn't lend its enchanting rays to our courtship. Beside Hamp had volunteered for any mission field and probably would have preferred South America. There was no conniving.

> The moon did not lend it's enchanting rays ever to our courtship, and it was done chiefly in the drawing room of the ship where the passengers surged thru at will, sometimes however we took

the top or hurricane deck and even the very prow one day. Nothing could have pleased us more than to have been in Tupelo in our own church and Bro. Dickenson perform the ceremony and bride accompanied by Miss Liv as maid of honor, Mer as matron, Little Gene, ring bearer, Olivia, Nannie, Clarice and so on maids. But the time was not ripe for it and even if he had felt inclined to ask me. I'd have laughed perhaps at the absurdity or at least said, 'no'. The first time he expressed any interest in me he said, 'I have a suspicion that I love you.' I blushed deeply, more or less surprised.

His eyes had told tales on him before. It seems that his Christian character and manly virtues played a part all along.

Without skipping a beat, she recounts the fact that Hamp's sister Viola from Charlotte, North Carolina, his brother and Mary his brother's wife from Winder, Georgia had all written; that Dr. Ware, Hamp's father, had written from Atlanta, and his Aunt Sallie Shellnut, his mother's sister who lived in Sandersville, Georgia, also had written. The pictures which Hamp and Mary Bibb had sent were not good at all.

Christmas gifts had already been opened and everyone was thanked individually for their presents. The week before Christmas had been used to decorate the house. The poinsettia and flowers sent by the Community Church were beautiful. They even had a small cedar tree with decoration sent from someone in Alabama. Bibb and Edith sang to the group before everyone dispersed to see others throughout the city. They had all put up stockings and everyone had packages to open. Breakfast was fruit instead of the usual waffles, and every one piled into the car and went to church where the children sang and Pastor Sung baptized four candidates. Bibb sat in Miss Priest's relining chair. After church everyone went to the Rawlingson's for lunch and heard stories about the past mission. By the time Bibb got home she was very tired; although people kept coming by to bring presents, she went to bed early.

Christmas didn't end on Christmas Day. Edith and Bibb put together a party. Hannah Plowden, Miss Paterson, Mrs. Rogers and Mr. and Mrs. Steel came to lunch and they all shared in an incredible dinner with tomato bisque and cheese straws. turkey with water-chestnut dressing, grapes, Irish potatoes, asparagus, beans from Union Town, Alabama, jelly sauce, fruit salad, plum pudding, hard sauce with peanuts and pecans, coffee, candy fruit and pudding. Christmas on the mission fields was a real celebration, particularly in Shanghai where almost everything was available.

Bibb did some gossiping of her own at the end of the letter. Everyone thinks that Hannah and Mr. Jackson will be getting married, but this is not to be repeated because it is uncertain. "Everyone in China knows more about your affairs than you do yourself, as she (Hannah) may not want it known. There is one time in your life that you let your light shine- that is if you come to China nothing is hid."

The last letter of the year ends with her expressed joy over Papa feeling better and the hope that Mer will get some help for the housework in Tupelo. She is so happy that

CHAPTER FIVE

Rue Lafayette 1922

Independent women have been a hallmark of my mother's family for generations. Bibb was no exception to the rule. The years leading up to her life in China were expressions of independence. Bibb's life was filled with women who broke the mold and expectations of southern culture at the beginning of the twentieth century. Not only had she graduated from Old Miss, The University of Mississippi, in a predominately male class, but she was also friends with independent women at Blue Mountain College, a Baptist women's college in North Mississippi. She had numerous friends in the Women's Missionary Union, the Baptist Women's Missionary Union, and the Women's Missionary Union Training School where she attended before she went to the mission field. In China her primary work was with both women missionaries and eventually with Chinese women. At Old North Gate church, Eliza Yates Girls School, and in her own bible school, her primary interest was in teaching and training independent women.

Some of Bibb's closet friends were taken back with her marriage to Hamp. In January Nineteen Twenty Two she received a letter from Nancy (her last name is missing), a friend at Old Miss. Nancy chides her for marrying Hamilton, especially since she had not told any of her friends at the University of Mississippi. In fact Bibb seems to have asserted her independence at Old Miss, and even declared that she would not ever get married. There were several people who were put out with her marriage, including Cousin Fanny Ware (no kin to Hamp). In the days before women's "lib", Bibb was a stanch supporter of women's independence. I think that this was largely due to her mother, "The General", who was an extremely strong and independent woman. In China she had role models in Miss Willey Kelly and Miss Priest. Actually the mission field was full of examples of independent women. Bibb kept her contacts at Blue Mountain and in the Women's Missionary Union all of her life. She nurtured them, and they nurtured her.

Nancy's letter was the first indication of Bibb's attitude toward marriage before she left for China on the Hawkeye. In her letter Nancy thanks Bibb for a string of pearls which she has received from China, and then proceeds to good naturedly chastise Bibb for going against her previously declared statement not to marry. Nancy teases, "I have not quite forgiven Mr. James Hamilton yet for walking off with my Bibb without so much as 'by Nancy's leave'. He evidently did not think that necessary; and, you are, after all, the one with whom the fault lies. (sic)" It seems that at some point Bibb had promised that she would not be "talked over" by a "mere man"; or, Nancy says, ". . .if you did, you would let me know before you took the rash step – after I say all these solemn promises, you write me a note and mention casually that you have 'a secret', and that 'he, etc.' As if I intuitively knew who 'he' was!" Nancy quits teasing Bibb and remarks that she is very pleased that Hamilton changed his station rather than taking her to North China.

Winter in Shanghai was unsually cold. It was not that a cold wind always blew in from Siberia, or that there was constant snow and ice. It was just misty cold dampness that seemed to seep through your cloths. Everything seemed to be wet like there had been a heavy dew. Your feet were always cold, and after you had been outside for a while, your nose inevitably ran. The schools and churches had little or no heat, and the houses had small hearths that held about a bucket of coal and never seemed to stay very warm, much less warm a whole room.

I remember very well the cold winters of 1947-1948. Thousands of refugees from North China, fleeing the Civil War, came to Shanghai, and there was no one to feed them, house them, or give them work. They slept in alleys and doorways wrapping their bodies with old newspapers, or what ever else they could find to get out of the penetrating cold. Many of them froze to death during the night. Each morning the city sent trucks around looking for the dead. The bodies were thrown on top of each other in the bed of the truck and taken out of the city to a common grave where they were often dumped, and bulldozers covered them up with dirt. Nineteen twenty two was nothing like that. The city was cold, but there was not the burden of thousands of homeless refugees.

Bibb's first letter of the year to Mer was written January sixth. It included a note written by Hamp thanking Mer for the letter of welcome into the Tupelo family. There was some concern in the family as to what to call him: Jim, Hamp, Hamilton, J.H. or James.

Hamp's reply was that his name in the family Bible was James Theodore Hamilton Carter Ware, and that they could choose the name they liked the best. He had, as a fact, already dropped the Theodore and Carter names when he was in college.

It had been long enough since the wedding that Hamp and Bibb were receiving wedding presents from the U.S. There were pictures of Hamp's mother and father sent by Myrtle Sturdivant, his cousin, a silver pie knife from the Farley's, and a set of Roger's 1847 silver place setting from "Father Ware." Because mission dinners often included everyone in the mission, Bibb asked her mother to send her six extra knives and forks.

There seems to have been some question as to whether Hamp and Bibb would remain in Shanghai. Dr. Ray, his wife and daughter, and his secretary Leite Hill had arrived on their way to Canton, and were staying at the Baptist College. A two day mission meeting for the central China Mission was to be held while Ray was in Shanghai. There were all sorts of decisions being made about policies and personnel. Hamp assured the mission that, although his first assignment by the Foreign Mission Board was to Hwangshien, he was staying in Shanghai, even though Dr. Ray wanted him to go to Hwangshien.

The mission confirmed Hamp's transfer from Hwangshien, but there was a question whether both of them might serve in Yangchou, a city on the Grand Canal further inland. The executive Committee finally decided that Bibb would continue her work, and Hamp would be a city missionary and head up the work of evangelism for the Shanghai group, and particularly follow up the work that had been started in the outstations. The out station assignment was to be temporary, but it became definitive of his missionary work until World War II. Bibb thought that her work might change since they needed a woman to work in the outstations as well as a man. Chapels were being built almost yearly by wealthy Chinese members of the churches, and these were served by both Chinese pastors and Hamp.

The meeting of the Central China Mission gave Hamp and Mary Bibb a chance to meet the missionaries from Soochow, Chinkyang, Yangchow, and Wu Shih. These people would be friends for life, the Olives, the Stamps, the McDaniels, the MacMillans, and Misses Lanneau, Grove, and Olive. There were some new faces as well as old friends. It is interesting to note that the other people they met, with the exception of the Tatums and Miss Demarest, did not spend their lives on the mission field. At that time no one thought that Misses Pierce and Marriott, Dr. and Mrs. Jordan, Misses Andrews and Teal would spend only a few years in China. The mission meeting was not all work; everyone took their own lunch and each day there was a picnic.

The most consequential and controversial decision made at the mission meeting was the removal of the Rawlingsons after twenty years of service. The Rawlingsons were accused of unorthodox teaching (which was unspecified) and union work. Dr. Rawlingson was highly respected by the other members of the mission for his intellectual ability. The missionaries in the mission gave the Rawlingsons a hundred United States dollar gift and a tea as a farewell present. They seemed to be very appreciative. Given the fact that senior missionaries usually work alone, it would be very interesting to know in what way Dr. Rawlingson was unorthodox, and how it had become an issue after twenty years. Bibb does not explain. Dr. Ray and his family left for Canton on the fourteenth. His secretary did not go with them.

Probably the most troubling event of the early year was not the mission meeting, but the death of two small girls, whom Bibb had gotten to know. They died within a week of each other. The smaller one died of scarlet fever in less than two days, and the older one, who had been in the North Gate Church School for nine years, died unexpectedly of unknown causes. It really disturbed Bibb that the older girl, Wang Pao Rau, had been in the school with them nine years and had not made a profession of faith. The girl was an aristocratic looking young woman. She was the daughter of a former pastor.

Several days after the girl's death, Bibb went to visit Mrs. Wang, the mother of the older girl, and found her quite beside herself. She was afraid of loosing her mind. In a typical manner for non-Christians, Mrs. Wang had taken a picture of the girl's head and had made a cardboard body for it. She had dressed the manikin in beautiful, elegant cloths. The image was then seated beside a table with books, a tea cup, and a vase of flowers, all beside a window with lace curtains. Bibb wrote, "Before the picture were two servants of paper to wait on her, a rice bowl, tea cup, or two rice bowls (sic), chop sticks, candles, incense burners, an urn that is kept burning for her.(sic) another man to light her candles and her tablet. On a stool near by were a wash pan full of water, cloths, tooth brushes, and glasses for her to use." Mrs. Wang came to school to see Miss Priest every few days and wept. Bibb was hopeful that she would convert.

Chinese New Year is just around the corner and everything is on hold for the Rue Lafayette compound. In her letter of January thirteenth Bibb still does not mention her birthday which was in December, but she complains about her appendicitis surgery. She can not wear her corset because she still feels bad.

Hamp and Bibb took their first language exam and now had two credits in Chinese. Hamp was far more proficient than Bibb, and would speak Chinese so well that even the Chinese will not be able to tell that he is not a native speaker.

It is the end of the school term and graduation exercises for the Chinese students are taking place. Many of the programs that the students put on are in English to show their ability and to show how much better their training was than those who attended the Confucian Schools. Valentine's Day was just around the corner, and Bibb tried to express her love for her Tupelo family in Chinese. She does fairly well. Her letter begun on January thirteenth is completed on the fourteenth. The weather is changing, getting much colder. She says that she wishes that Olivia would write more often, and gives her love to Sam, Big and

Little Gen, and to Grand, and signs off, "Your affectionate daughter". Bibb.

Edith Wisenhunt and Bibb are taking over the preparations and meals for the holidays, Valentine's and Chinese New Year, as Miss Kelly and Miss Priest have gone to Peking to have Miss Kelly's tonsils out at the Rockefeller Foundation Hospital. Bibb and Hamp celebrated their three month wedding anniversary. Although the weather was cold, this January seemed to have been pleasant. However, it did snow on January twenty eighth. Bibb lamented that they were not able to have snow ice cream because they did not know how clean the water was that made up the snow.

Dr. E.M. Poteet preached at the Community Church. And, it seems that Bibb was impressed with him, but Hamp said, "He got under his skin."

Chinese New Year was on the twenty eight, and the household help was given time off. The meals at Rue Lafayette were always good. Prices for items that had to be imported were fairly high; but, sweet potatoes were only 2½ cents, Irish potatoes 3-4 cents, oranges 10 cents, fresh tomatoes 8 cents, spinach 4 cents, best cuts of beef 25 cents a pound, mutton chops 30 cents, brains 5 cents a set, egg plant 5 cents a pound. Almost everything was paid in Chinese coppers, or in Mexican silver dollars (two Mexican dollars to one United States dollar). Although missionaries were not that well remunerated, their lives were not a hardship as far as food was concerned.

Although things were not that expensive Bibb and Hamp had to make some choices. When two movies, "Mrs.

Wiggins of the Cabbage Patch" and "The Last of the
Mohegan's", came to Shanghai, tickets were $ 1.00 and
$ 1.50 (Mex.) A choice had to be made whether to see
the movies or save the money for a memory or Kodak
photo album. Eventually they did see "Mrs. Wiggins of the
Cabbage Patch". It was the first motion picture they saw in
China, and unfortunately they did not like it at all.

Bibb not only wrote to her mother, but also to her brother
Sam and his wife Gene. On Chinese New Year she went
into a long explanation of the customs of the day. Chinese
New Year's Day was the only day that everyone put aside
work and played. The fireworks and music kept them
awake all night. It was also a day of reckoning with any
one who owed someone else money. Bibb explains the role
of the Kitchen God, who looked after the family all year
and made his report on New Year's Day. She explained
that the Kitchen God, which was a scroll hung up in the
kitchen, had his mouth smeared with honey so that his
report would be good. He was then seated in a paper sedan
chair, and was burned in order to send him up to heaven to
make his report. For the next few days there is no Kitchen
God hanging in the house and people caroused as they
pleased, and they visited the family grave mound. When
I was growing up, more than a quarter of the land around
our compound was taken up with grave mounds. We lived
just outside the city and some of the grave mounds were
quite large and twenty or more feet high. Generation had
been buried there on top of each other.

One day during the New Years festival several of the
missionaries gathered at the Hipp's house at the Shanghai
Baptist College, later to be known as Shanghai University,

in English and Wu Kong Da Ah (The Wu Dialect College), in Chinese. The college had drained a pond and Dr. White, the President, had sold the fish from the pond for two hundred Mexican dollars. The cook, who had bought them, sold them again for a thousand Mexican dollars, plus feeding some of the students. Shanghai University was a joint enterprise between Northern and Southern Baptist. The University was very unusual in that it was co-educational. It had a women's dormitory and a normal school for children. The science building, not only cost over a hundred thousand United States' dollars, it was exceptionally well equipped.

Hamp and Bibb are already looking forward to the summer. They plan to go to Chinkiang by train and then by boat up the Grand Canal to the mountain resort at Kuling. They will get out of the Shanghai heat, but not out of their work. Their teacher will go with them. The Stamps, Shields, and Wisenhunts will go also. They will all rent a house and share expenses. The Wisenhunts will go in spite of the fact that they have begun building a home in Shanghai.

Bibb ends her last letter of January by saying they have gotten a bunch of letters, and had a good cry. Hamp has been so good to her; especially when she got nostalgic and weepy. He is too good to be true.

January has passed. Letter writing has become problematic because the local sailors have gone on strike. However, the pace of things has not slowed down. Miss Priest has returned from Peking. Miss Kelly had her dental work completed, but stayed for some extra medical help. Bibb has paid her hospital bill; but Dr. Hiltner has not sent his bill for the appendectomy. She and Hamp seem to have enough money; they told Mer that they did not need help. They would pay off Hiltner's bill twenty five dollars a month. All of the cloths and other items that Hamp had left in Peking finally arrived. Some items were either lost or stolen. Even his extra pair of glasses was missing.

It appears that some of the women at the American Women's Club had gone crazy playing Mahjong, and a group of Chinese have strongly disapproved of it because of its association with gambling. The Chinese were not unaware of American social activities; approval and disapproval were strong factors in missionary life. One of the nicer things that happened was that the women of the First Baptist Church in Tupelo named their circle after Mary Bibb. Life in Tupelo went on. Olivia finished High School and Bibb wanted her to go to Blue Mountain College. Instead she chose Mary Hardin Baylor.

Life at Rue Lafayette was good. Hamp and Bibb made some divinity out of plain syrup (there was no karo) and pecans that Hawthorn had sent. Bibb got sentimental over her mother's birthday and wrote a long poem about how her mother had helped her to grow up. Bibb always ended her letters by sending her love to all of the neighbors in Tupelo.

People were always coming and going. Bibb's final letter of the month tells about seeing Miss Todd off and how they all pitched coins off the pier into the water for the beggars to dive after.

February gave way to March and a spring garden. Sadness had struck at Shanghai College. Mrs. Westbrook had dies of cholera and Miss Keathly had made it through, but was still very ill. Word had also come that Father Ware was sick with something called acid blood. Bibb was homesick and depressed until a flood of letters arrived in late March. Father Ware was better and everything was going well in Shanghai. Dr. Ray passed through on the way home, and before he left threw a big party on the boat on which he was traveling. By the end of March Bibb's spirits seemed much better,

Both she and Hamp had their sensibilities challenged one day when they found a yellow box on the curb just across the street from the driveway on Rue Lafayette. Inside was a child, several days old that had been abandoned and had died. They turned the package over to the police. This experience of finding an abandoned baby on the street happened numerous times, especially during the later war years.

Missionaries in China often had different visions of their work. In spite of the missionaries' differences the Chinese Christians tended to be more open to one another. Bibb wrote to her mother that Old North Gate Church, which was hosting pre-Easter services for the Chinese Christian community, served open communion, i.e. anyone having been baptized into any church, was invited to the communion table to partake. Bibb felt that the Y.M.C. A. was most responsible for this practice. And states: "I believe it will be the means of bringing many unregenerate young men into the Church." She does not have time to elaborate on why she feels this way toward the Y.M.C.A.;

consequently she did not want her mother to repeat what she had written.

Not much correspondence between Bibb and Mer was saved during March, but it picks up sharply in April. Olivia is graduating from High School and Bibb wants her to have a Japanese silk kimono, which is very expensive. Bibb nevertheless gets the kimono. Nothing of consequence happens the rest of the month. Spring has come and the flowers are beautiful, especially the wisteria, azaleas, and snow balls.

After Hamp's and Bibb's experience of the abandoned child, Miss Kelly decides that they should be introduced to the Door of Hope, an orphanage which two German women had established for abandoned children. The Door of Hope ran on donations; it did not have any source of permanent backing. Some of the older girls there knitted sweaters for some of the foreigners, but contributions were their primary source of funding.

Events change rapidly. On April twenty fifth Bibb reports that she has had a "villainous attack." She writes:

> I could enthusiastically wish that the present evil be the fore runner of the greatest pleasure and blessing I know of in the life of a mere women, and I may be. . . but I don't think so. I missed my period this month which is very unusual for me. . . Mother Dear, you would be astonished if you knew how little I knew about new life before I was married. . . . I never gave you a chance to talk to me because of false modesty or timidity, but I

believe every girl ought to know and regard most sacred the mystery of life.

There is a second part to Bibb's April twenty fifth letter which she marked "Private and Personal." She had been over to Mrs. Bill's, who helped her make a list of things she would need if she were pregnant. Mrs. Bills had three children; two born in China. Bibb wanted her mother to send her three silk and wool shirts, four bands, two dozen diapers, four pairs of silk and wool stockings and some rubber sheeting for a play pen, or "kitty koop" and buggy. She will pay for these things when she knows the price. Bibb has already determined that she will go to a hospital to have the baby. Nurses are inexpensive. Both she and Hamp have already been making plans and building children's toys and beds. They have determined that the baby will come on Christmas day or the following day.

Bibb is concerned about her health and her overpowering desire to stay in bed. Her weight is good, but she still needs to be out of bed. She has noticed a discharge and is afraid of a miscarriage. She admits to Mer, "I never have wanted to be with you so much in my life- I don't like to talk to folks out here for they talk so freely to others." She wants to be prepared for a premature arrival, and almost wished that they were not going to Kuling.

On May First Bibb had trouble keeping food down, and was in bed much of the time. Uncharacteristically, Hamp is worried enough to add his take on things to a letter Bibb had written to her mother. He was worried and depressed. Finally Bibb and Hamp resorted to Dr. Hiltner, in spite of his rather high fees. The problem broke the next day. Bibb not only felt better, she was hungry and eating. According to their letter of May fifteenth, Bibb is in Fearn Hospital for a number of days. Dr. Hiltner thinks that part of Bibb's problem is that she is studying too hard. But, he is also sure that she is pregnant. She confesses in her letter to her mother that she didn't care whether she lived or died during the days when she was so sick. Hamp has been very attentive. He even slept on the floor two nights while she was so sick. She is quite taken by his solicitations and even says, "I never saw anyone who is more like the Master in his heart and life." Of course Hamp's sister, Viola's experience of being unable to have children and Mary's and Hawthorn's loss of their child are on both Hamp's and Mary Bibb's mind. The two of them speculate about the baby; both of them want a girl, but they would cherish a boy, if things turned out that way.

Bibb's recovery at Fearn Hospital is measured. She takes a little water, but does not keep down any thing else. However, by the nineteenth she is ready to go home to Rue Lafayette Not everything is going well there either. The cook and the amah are at each other's throats. They have to let the cook go to restore peace. The Wisenhunts are unhappy with Miss Kelly; they felt like she is trying to run their lives. Bibb recognized Miss Kelly's domineering character and says that she simply puts up with it because Miss Kelly is accustomed to having her way at Old North Gate. The house is full, every room is in use, and make shift accommodations are made for others.

By May twenty fourth Bibb is much better, although she stays in bed most of the time. Dr. Hiltner is giving her some form of injection twice a week. Back at Rue Lafayette she goes down stairs for meals and occasionally goes to visit friends; but, by in large her activities are limited. Her primary gripe is that everyone knows her business and is talking about it. She actually gets angry thinking about it.

As Bibb gets better, she gets more demonstrative about the baby's coming .In her letters to her mother Bibb begins to talk about their impending trip to Kuling. They will sail up the Yangtze in Chinese First Class on a Japanese ship. She and Hamp will need to carry their own food, bedding, and mosquito netting on the ship. Fortunately, Bibb's hospital bill at Dr. Fearus was less than expected and the cost of the boat was half of what they had anticipated. There was enough left for Bibb and Hamp to buy a portable typewriter (about 120.00 dollars) which will help both of them.

Although Bibb begins to feel better, she still spends a great deal of time in bed, however, her interests are broader, and she is beginning to think in terms of her missionary work. One of the interests which she has apart from Old North Gate Church is a chapter of the Women's Christian Temperance Union. The Chinese are not involved in the W.C.T.U., but it is an important group as far as Bibb is concerned. Up until Olivia's birth Bibb's father, Judge Long, had been a heavy drinker. It was not until after Olivia birth that he stopped cold turkey.

Dr. Hiltner gives his opinion that Bibb is now able to travel. There is plenty of medical help in Kuling, and there is no reason why they should not go. Preparations are made to cross over the Yangtze River at about four o'clock and send their baggage to the other side by sampan. The

Mabies will be on this boat also, so they will have traveling companions. Their address in Kuling will be 215 B. Bibb hopes there will be mail for them from Tupelo when they get there.

The trip to Kuling is far more than they expect. Miss Graves from Shanghai Baptist College is on board, as are two Asian women. Bibb is not able to tell whether they are Japanese or Chinese, which seems a bit odd since she has been in China for a year now. Traveling up the river is very smooth; it is almost as if the boat were standing still. The only noise is water passing under the boat. Along the bank are several floating villages. At one point there is a man getting water out of the river by means of a rope and wooden bucket. At another place they see their first pagoda; it is seven stories high, painted white, trimmed in red, and has windows on each level. Around a turn in the river they see Anking and the Episcopal mission there. Two women board the ship there and they all proceed up the river. On either side of the river there are villages with straw thatched roofs. Water buffalo and cows work the fields along the river. Trees along the river are short and scrubby, and far away in the distance the mountains rise on the horizon. Sometimes the tops of the mountain are hidden in clouds. Kuling and the surrounding mountains are about three thousand five hundred feet above sea level. Many of the banks of the river are covered in red bud and other shrubs. Bibb is surprised not to have seen any large bamboo. What is significant about Bibb's account is that she has been in China for over a year and yet these common ordinary scenes are new to her. She has not had the experiences that Hamp has had. He traveled from

Tsingtao to Peking and then to Shanghai and saw a large portion of North Eastern China.

On Saturday, they arrived across the river from Kuling during a down pour. The boat anchored, and the party took a small boat across the river to the foot of Kuling Mountain. The rest of the way they took sedan chairs, carried by four Chinese, up the mountain to house 215 B. The Kuling Association owned and operated the resort so that the only expense they had was to pay was the servants. Kuling was beautiful. There were daisies, lilies, and wild flowers everywhere. The next day Bibb is uncharacteristically active, and walked down the mountain two times. The second day they were there they were involved in a baseball game. Kuling was an ideal place for young missionaries. There were tennis courts, baseball fields, walking paths, streams, and small lakes where they could fish. After a morning of study, there were often lectures and religious services conducted by other missionaries and scholars who were invited as guests. The guests often put on plays for the other missionaries and held concerts for one another.

Kuling not only has the mountain, but it also has large flowing lakes near by, There are picnics almost every week. Bibb was ecstatic and Hamp was thoroughly enjoying himself. Bibb seems to have only had two or three bad days while they were there. Hamp writes to Mother Long that Bibb is as happy and well as she has been in China. She is doing very well in their studies largely due to her buoyed spirits. Hamp hopes that their second year is China will be much better that the first.

One of primary events of the up and coming central China mission meeting is the decision to sell all the current Shanghai properties and buy one big compound. A decision will also be made concerning a house for the Wares. Both of them are looking forward to a home of their own. Hamp concludes his letter to Mother Long telling her to continue giving Bibb advice. It seems she does not take advice from anyone else very well. Before they leave Kuling Bibb and Hamp make out wills. It seems that without a will, the American consulate will take all of their possessions when they die, process them, and charge them for the entire operation. Neither one of them want this to happen.

Kuling is not far from a number of mission stations and Hamp and Bibb take advantage of the opportunity to visit some of the inland missionaries. The time arrives to leave Kuling, and they begin the trip down the Yangtze River to Shanghai. Things are not too good at Rue Lafayette. Miss Kelly is sick, and the cook is too sick to carry out his responsibility. They all agree to let the cook go, but there is no one there to take his place. Edith and Bibb substitute until they find another cook.

All along in Kuling Bibb is rather proud of herself for not showing. She has had such a good time. With only a few days when she felt poorly, she expects the rest of her term of carrying their baby will go well. However, in just a few days she is rudely turned around. She begins to have back pains and a discharge. She goes to Dr. Hilton, who is certain that she had had a miscarriage, and that the current discharge is a return of her body to its proper state. She is back to her normal menstrual cycle. Of course this is hard for her to take. She feels sick, and she will feel sick for the next three years.

Bibb continues her studies, but she only does token work at Old North Gate Church, and that is with children. She has not really learned how to relate to adult Chinese. Miss Kelly asks her and Hamp to prepare segments of the 1922-23 report of North Gate Church and they both do the job rather well. But it is Hamp who actually relates to the Chinese and gets his work going.

There is a second Mrs. J.H. Ware in Shanghai, who neither Hamp nor Bibb ever meets. She, unfortunately dies, and Hamp receives all sorts of condolences from people who think that Bibb is the person who has died. What has died with Bibb is enthusiasm. Everything is not the same. She later refers to the next few years as the period of her illness. She goes to a women chiropractor, Dr. Cooper, and js helped some with her back; but she simply does not have the same enthusiasm. Her letters begin to be totally focused on Tupelo, especially on Olivia and Little Gene. Although she says that she is determined to do what God would want her to do, she is far less energetic doing it. In October Bibb writes that Dr. Hiltner says that she is in pretty good shape, that there is nothing wrong except some minor irritation, and he is giving her some medicine for that.

Hamp and Bibb celebrate their first wedding anniversary in late October. Bibb wears her wedding dress, and they have friends over for dinner. Miss Kelly has been sick. At first they thought it was cholera. But, they took her to the hospital in an ambulance and found out it was simply an intestinal bug. Miss Priest is holding down the fort at Rue Lafayette, and the transition of servants is basically complete.

Bibb's November letter congratulates her father for winning his election to the judgeship of the First District Circuit Court in Mississippi, and she sends him a poem to mark his success.

A few days later Bibb is back in the hospital and Dr. Hiltner is doing a curetting. She is not very happy about being in the hospital and is not looking forward to having to take ether. This hospital is not all that comfortable; the two nurses at the Victoria Nursing Home who attend her are Caucasian. Bibb's stay at the nursing home is a bit longer than anticipated. Dr. Hiltner brought his little three year old daughter to visit Bibb .He was taking care of her because his wife had died two years before. Unfortunately, he had put Vaseline in the child's hair the day before and couldn't get it all out.

Bibb's health is fairly good in spite of her surgery. She weighs a hundred and thirty five pounds, a bit more than Hamp. It is time to go home after the third trip to the hospital. Her Chinese teacher is terribly disturbed because of her surgery. Bibb seems to think that Chinese are afraid of surgery, and that Mr. Sie, in particular, is troubled. When Bibb is ready to go home, she goes by ambulance; and, when she gets home, she rests for another five days. Through out her ordeal Bibb is not focused on herself but on Tupelo and the well being of everyone there. She does not seem to be able to get her mind off her father, brothers, Julia, Olivia, Little Gene, and, of course Mer. She keeps talking about God's will, but she doesn't seem to be able to let her anxiety go. Hamp tries to help; he even carries her down stairs for her meals. He does not linger around the house, but stays busy at Old North Gate Church and keeps looking for land for the mission.

The last letter that has survived from the year 1922 was begun on November the twenty ninth and added on to for the next several days. During the first of December Father Ware writes several letters to Hamp about his Aunt Mary Sue, his mother's sister. She is in the Georgia State Hospital in Milledgeville and clearly mentally ill. Unfortunately his father is not able to do anything about her situation. He is tied up with one of the best crops of any year that he can remember, and he hopes to get it in before it spoils.

Probably the best source of information for the end of the year for Bibb comes from Miss Priest and Miss Kelly. Both of them write encouraging notes to Mer. According to Miss Priest, Bibb has undergone this ordeal with a cheerful spirit, and although Bibb has cried when she realized that the little cloths that she had made would not be used, never the less "the tears were of the April shower variety, the sunshine and jokes following soon after". Of course Hamp was the best nurse Bibb could have had. He is an extra ordinary person. Miss Priest relates how he was called on to pray at Old North Gate Church and prayed a long and meaningful prayer in Chinese. It impressed everyone.

Bibb's friends are going to give her a surprise party for her birthday. They are planning on quite a party – orange cake, chicken salad, hot biscuits, sandwiches, coffee, tea, and peaches with whipped cream. Miss Kelly wrote only a post card on December twenty ninth. However. it reassures Mer about Bibb's health, and then retells of the party that they are having for Bibb.

So ends 1922, the beginning of the story of Hamp and Mary Bibb. Bibb will change. She will have three children and she will begin to identify with Chinese women. Hamp will establish a large number of out stations and serve numerous functions in the Central China Mission. Both of them will undergo the Japanese occupation of Shanghai, and see the Communists take over Mainland China.

Printed in the United States
By Bookmasters